James Britten

Protestant fiction

Second Edition

James Britten

Protestant fiction

Second Edition

ISBN/EAN: 9783741191763

Manufactured in Europe, USA, Canada, Australia, Japa

Cover: Foto ©Thomas Meinert / pixelio.de

Manufactured and distributed by brebook publishing software (www.brebook.com)

James Britten

Protestant fiction

PROTESTANT FICTION

BY

JAMES BRITTEN, K.S.G.,

HON. SEC. CATHOLIC TRUTH SOCIETY

CENTRAL CIRCULATION

LONDON
CATHOLIC TRUTH SOCIETY
69 SOUTHWARK BRIDGE ROAD, S.E.
1899

CONTENTS.

	PAGE
INTRODUCTORY .	v
I. NUNS . . .	1
II. THE JESUITS . .	33
III. PRIESTS . . .	65
IV. THE LAITY	97
V. PROTESTANT POETS . . .	129

INTRODUCTION.

TOWARDS the end of 1895 some papers which had been written for *The Month*, under the title " Protestant Fiction," were reprinted as a volume. The thousand copies thus published were speedily exhausted, and I have been asked to reissue the book in a cheaper form. The chapters, as now published, have been revised, and a good deal of new matter has been added.

The books dealt with are for the most part avowedly works of fiction, having for their aim the propagation of Protestant views concerning the Catholic Church. I am well aware that my title is equally applicable to a vast number of books of Protestant controversy, such as Dr. Littledale's *Plain Reasons against Joining the Church of Rome;* Mr. Lancelot Holland's *Walled Up and Walled In;* the works of Dr. Grattan Guinness; the publications of the Protestant Alliance, especially those written by Mr. C. H. Collette; the preposterous narratives, professing to be records of fact, of which *Maria Monk* is the prototype and certain pamphlets published by Mr. John Kensit are the most recent examples. Works of this class have the strongest claims to be included in any exhaustive treatment of Protestant Fiction, and some of them are quoted in these pages; but they do not form the staple of the collection.

When these chapters are read, amusement and

amazement will probably be equally blended in the minds of those to whom Protestant literature of a certain class is unfamiliar. To these feelings, indignation will doubtless succeed; but the sentiment which must finally prevail will be one of pity for the extraordinary misconception of Catholic faith and practice which characterises the publications here passed under notice. It is wellnigh incredible that ignorance which the perusal of the Penny Catechism or a conversation with a Catholic would at once dispel, should be possible at the present day; but the evidence adduced is more than sufficient to show that to a section of our fellow-countrymen the teaching and practice of the greater part of Christendom is absolutely unknown.

It is true that by one means or another, and especially owing to the work of the High Church party in the Establishment, our countrymen during the last fifty years have greatly advanced in the knowledge of things Catholic. It is equally true that a large proportion of those who calumniate us are paid officials of societies, whose occupation would be gone were the Church pourtrayed in her true colours, and whose interest it is to foster and develop popular prejudice against us. One such society, as *Truth* pointed out,[1] was formed by Mr. John Kensit, who is its sole officer, for the express purpose of promoting the sale of his publications, many of which, on the authority of the same non-Catholic organ of opinion, are an outrage upon decency. But the number of men of influence and independence who support these

[1] 11th January, 1894.

Introduction. vii

bodies is not only small, but decreasing; any one familiar with the reports of anti-Catholic meetings published in Protestant papers, will notice the constant repetition of the same names, and these of persons in no way representing English opinion.

On the other hand, it must be remembered that certain men of undoubted position are not ashamed to be associated with the "lewd fellows of the baser sort" who are the self-constituted champions of Protestantism. Dean Farrar and the Rev. H. E. Fox, Secretary of the Church Missionary Society, think it no shame to patronize the same publisher who is responsible for the publications denounced by *Truth*. Each of these representative members of the Established Church has had his attention called to the company he is keeping, and neither has dissociated himself from it.

I am frequently asked where I found the material on which these chapters are based, and it seems to be thought that I have taken considerable pains to bring it together. But it abounds on all sides. The grosser fictions, indeed, emanate from Mr. Kensit's shop and from Racquet Court; but respectable bodies like the Religious Tract Society, eminent publishers like the Messrs. Longman, philanthropic organisations like the Pure Literature Society, high-placed ecclesiastics like Dean Farrar, leading Nonconformists like Dr. Horton, are not ashamed to put forward publications as inaccurate and misleading, although not so offensive, as the works of Dr. Fulton and General Sir Robert Phayre. A mere glance through the names of those from whom I have quoted will show that clergymen (both Anglican and Nonconformist), lawyers, military men, women of education and social position, contribute to swell the tide of Protestant misrepresentation which vainly rages and swells round the Rock on which the Church is founded. The difficulty has not been in the finding, but in the selection of material; I have not even referred to one-fourth of the stories devoted to attacks on Catholicism which are in my possession, and which I have picked up, for the most part, on bookstalls or in the " fourpenny box ".

Prejudice and ignorance, as Cardinal Newman has pointed out in a masterly manner in his *Lectures on the Present Position of Catholics in England*, are the main supports of the Protestant tradition. Both are difficult to overcome, yet both have to some extent been vanquished among the more educated classes of the community. It is well known that habits of mind and practice, like the fashions, descend from the higher to the lower grades of society; and the Protestant tradition singularly exemplifies this. Nothing is more striking than the want of ordinary literary capability in the aggressive portion of the Protestant press, unless it be the absence of influential names from the list of writers. Take the Protestant works which are quoted in these chapters, the monthly and weekly Protestant papers, or even the reports of the Protestant societies—everywhere one is struck with the same curious construction of sentences, the same confusion of ideas. Among the Protestant lecturers, the men of any weight or influence may be numbered on the fingers of one hand; while some are of by no means doubtful antecedents. Experience has not taught our antagonists to be careful: the disappearance of one, the imprisonment of another, the exposure

Introduction. ix

of a third, fail to impress upon them the necessity of caution. They still plant in their gardens, as flowers of great price, the weeds which the Pope has flung over his garden-wall. The Rev. Oswald Keatinge, Dr. Hammond, Brother Alphonse, Dr. Fulton, and other "lewd fellows of the baser sort," have appeared and disappeared with phenomenal rapidity—they went up like rockets, and came down like the sticks. Five years ago Miss Ellen Golding, the "Rescued Nun," was a power on the Protestant platform: what has become of her?

Yet "Amurath to Amurath succeeds," and since the disappearance of those I have named, the Protestant Alliance has stood sponsor for "the Rev. Joseph Slattery" and the woman who travels with him under the name of "Sister Mary Elizabeth," although their disreputable antecedents were well known, and had been completely exposed, before they ever set foot in this country. Yet Protestants extended to them a hearty welcome; and even so scandalous a person as "the Rev. Victor M. Ruthven" succeeded for a time in rousing anti-Catholic feeling and in obtaining support from the credulous. Even now "the Rev. F. G. Widdows," fresh from a sentence of ten years' penal servitude for a disgraceful offence, attracts large audiences to his lectures, which seem to consist of indecency and buffoonery in about equal proportions.

At times one is inclined to despair: but it cannot always be thus. The Anglican movement has, at any rate, done much to familiarize Englishmen with Catholic beliefs and practices; and among the Church of England clergy, the supporters of the more intense

b

forms of Protestantism are neither numerous nor influential. I shall be reminded that the Dean of Canterbury is one of them, and I may be asked whether I include him among those who are ignorant of Catholicism. I answer, Yes; and I do so because it is the only ground on which his attitude towards the Church can charitably be accounted for.

Forty-five years have passed since Cardinal Newman published the Lectures to which I have already referred; and although the ignorance which he therein describes has in some quarters been dispelled, in others it remains. Whether it is culpable, we are not called upon to judge; but we are all bound to do our best to enlighten it. For it may still be said of some of our countrymen that "in this inquisitive age, when the Alps are crested, and seas fathomed, and mines ransacked, and sands sifted, and rocks cracked into specimens, and beasts caught and catalogued, as little is known by Englishmen of the religious sentiments, the religious usages, the religious motives, the religious ideas of 200,000,000 Christians poured to and fro among them and around them, as if, I will not say they were Tartars or Patagonians, but as if they inhabited the moon. Verily, were the Catholic Church in the moon, England would gaze on her with more patience, and delineate her with more accuracy than England does now."

It is manifestly the duty of every Catholic to do his utmost to dispel the darkness which still encompasses many of his fellow-countrymen; and this can be done by spreading the knowledge of the Church as she really is, and by confuting the false statements which are made concerning her. There is no lack of

Introduction. xi

literature specially written with these two ends in view. The Catholic Truth Society has provided a series of cheap and useful leaflets and pamphlets explanatory of Catholic faith and practice, with others in which the popular calumnies against the Church are refuted. Not only "by kindly word and virtuous life," but by the promulgation of every means in our power of the truth as God has revealed it to His Church, must we work for the restoration of the "faith of our fathers" to the land which has so long been estranged from the Catholic unity.

Feast of St. Gregory, 1899.

PROTESTANT FICTION.

I. NUNS AND CONVENTS.

I HAVE selected as a type of this class of Protestant Fiction a penny story published by S. W. Partridge & Co., Paternoster Row, entitled *St. Mary's Convent; or, Chapters in the Life of a Nun*, by "Jeanie Selina Dammast (Reeves)." It has attained its hundredth thousand, and is now reprinting: this will give some idea of the enormous circulation reached by these stories. There is a striking picture on the cover of a nun kneeling in a garden, which I cannot connect with any incident in the tale; apart from this there are no illustrations. I proceed to epitomize the story, using, as far as possible, the words of the author.

Captain Seward, who had retired on half-pay, was travelling in Spain for the benefit of his health. But in this aim he was disappointed.

Before many weeks an attack of ague and fever reduced him to the weakness of an infant; and he was taken care of by the monks of a monastery near which he had become ill, and tended as if he were a Brother, instead of the heretic that they discovered him to be from his ravings during the fever. For many weeks the Brothers of St. Joseph were assiduous in their attentions; and, often as the languid invalid lay dreamily gazing on the dim twilight, a softly modulated strain of music, now breathing on the air, now swelling into bursts of harmonious sound, would come stealing through the cloisters, and die gradually away, filling the whole soul with its melting cadences, and subduing the stern soldier's heart beneath its influence, until unrestrained tears flowed from his eyes. As he became better, he loved to take his place in a dark corner of the convent chapel, and listen to the solemn chanting of the monks; and, one memorable evening, when the Mass for the Dead was performed with all its accompanying ceremonial of incense and requiems, his soul yielded to the subduing influence of the scene, and, to the joy of the monks, who had carefully noted every change and phase of feeling in their guest, and suited their plans to it, he sank among the worshippers, and from that hour was, if possible, a more zealous and devoted Roman Catholic than the most sincere among his hosts. Fasting and penance were for the present forbidden by the wily men who had led him on step by step to the profession of their faith; but his grief had found a means of assuaging itself in prayers for his dead wife, and nearly his whole time was spent either in the library or in the chapel, where, in a half-entranced state, he listened for hours to the deep tones of the organ pealing through the arched aisles, and the soft, flute-like notes of the acolytes floating like angel voices through the air, blending their thrilling sweetness with the deeper voices of the monks as they joined the swelling chorus.

This sketch shows a remarkable knowledge of the manners and customs of a Spanish monastery. It may perhaps be urged that Mass for the Dead is not usually "performed" in the evening, and that "all its accompanying ceremonial of incense and requiems" reads somewhat oddly. But it must be observed that the monks "suited their plans" to "every change and phase of feeling in their guest." No doubt it was obvious to them that a Mass in the evening, accompanied by "incense and requiems," was the one thing needed to ensure Captain Seward's conversion; and the event justified their anticipations.

But a jarring note broke across the flute-like melody of the acolytes. The Captain's sister, Mrs. Stanley, wrote to say that his daughter, Emily, had become engaged to her son. "The suddenness of the intimation roused his mind to a more than usual state of activity," and he consulted the Prior as to what should be done. The Prior very properly pointed out that the young people were "within the prohibited degrees," besides being Protestants, and urged Captain Seward to proceed at once to England. Whether the Captain's announcement that he had hoped to end his days in the monastery had anything to do with the Prior's anxiety for his departure, it is difficult to say; any way, the Captain started off, and in due course arrived at Mrs. Stanley's. The family were having tea on the lawn when he arrived. Mrs. Stanley, "in a commotion of sisterly and hospitable feeling," went to prepare a room for her brother, who had "driven Emily back into herself by the ceremonious salute he bestowed upon her." To his dismay, Captain Seward learned, not only that Emily's *fiancé* was going to become a parson, but that her "whole soul and feelings were deeply imbued with the spirit of Protestantism."

A fortnight dragged slowly by; and one morning at breakfast, after he had read a voluminous letter from Spain, Captain Seward announced that he must start next day for a distant part of the country, taking Emily with him. And start they did, in a post-chaise; Emily weeping unrestrainedly, while her father opened a book and read. "If she could have looked over his shoulder she would have seen with surprise that it was a Breviary." One only wonders it was not a Missal.

The voluminous letter which Captain Seward had received from Spain contained an introduction from the Prior to the parish priest at T———. T——— is in one of the most beautiful counties of Ireland, where there "stands a small mountain called, in the neighbourhood, emphatically, 'The Hill.'" Here, after "a weary journey of three days"—a fact which, coupled with the post-chaise, leads us to suspect that this is not a very recently written story—they arrived, and "here Captain Seward intended to open the campaign against his unsuspecting child." He at once went to call on the priest, who had also been written to by the Prior.

Emily was very much astonished to see her father on such intimate terms with a gentleman of whom she had never heard him speak; but her surprise was greatly increased when, on the first Sunday of their stay at T——, her father led her into the Roman Catholic house of worship instead of the Protestant one. Thinking he had made a mistake, she ventured to whisper to him: "Father, this is not our church." But with a warning gesture to her to desist from speaking, he fell on his knees, crossing himself (as it is called) in the most devout manner, and giving himself up entirely to the ceremony that was going on. Emily was greatly shocked and puzzled by this strange conduct, and at last a firm conviction took possession of her mind that grief and illness combined, had unsettled her father's intellect. This solution of the difficulty seemed also to cast a ray of light on all that had distressed and chilled her in his manner; and, trying to cheer herself with the hope that by love and care she might yet see him restored to perfect health and sanity, she sat watching his bowings and crossings with mingled pity and affection. Mr. Devine, the priest, had been invited to dine with them; and when Emily moved to retire after dinner, her father requested her to remain, saying he did not feel very well, and would go to his room for an hour. With all the ease and politeness of a man of the world, Mr. Devine led the conversation; and Emily was delighted with his varied information and the fund of thought and discrimination he brought to bear on men and things. By degrees the tone of the conversation altered; and, while entirely unable to account for how it had been brought about, Emily found herself deep in a theological argument, in which, while seeing the light, she

Nuns and Convents. 5

seemed to be feeling her way through a thick darkness that obscured her mental vision, and enabled the priest to say, as tea was announced, "You see, my dear young lady, you have been looking at things from a wrong point of view, and therefore your arguments, though skilfully put, cannot stand; but, with your fine intellect and quick powers of discernment, I feel assured you will not long continue to think as you now do."

Captain Seward having returned, the conversation became general, and nothing worthy of note took place that evening.

On the slope of the emphatic hill already mentioned was built the Convent of St. Mary, which certainly possesses attractive external features.

The house is a large, red-brick edifice, and it is surrounded by picturesque grounds, laid out in the most ornamental manner. Winding steps, cut in the rock, lead to terrace after terrace, where the most charming views of the surrounding country can be obtained; and grottoes and summer-houses afford rest and shelter. Flowers of every hue add to the beauty of the scene, and the song of the birds is heard from every tree; but the more lovely is the spot, so much the more is the restraint felt when you reach, on every side, high ungainly walls, that form a complete barrier to the outside world, so rich in beauty: the birds that sing so sweetly may fly over it, and continue their strain; but the poor black-robed nuns, who pace the prescribed limits, must sigh in vain for the delights of freedom. That large mansion, and those grounds so highly embellished, are in reality a prison, where the inmates are incarcerated, not for a few short months or irksome years, but for *life*;—a prison from which nothing can release them but that universal deliverer, *death*.[1]

[1] There is, however, as we learn from *The Protestant Woman* for October, 1895, another mode of escape. "The better kind of Roman Catholics themselves have a horror of [convents]. I remember saying once to a Roman Catholic officer some years ago, ' Do you think that a convent is a happy place for a young girl to enter ? ' He answered vehemently, ' I have a sister who is a nun, but I had rather she had died than take the veil.' A few years later an old lady, a friend of

To this convent, at Mr. Devine's invitation, Emily and her father bent their steps. Her first impressions were pleasing:—

Merry voices and ringing laughs were heard along the stairs and corridors, and groups of nuns and novices were seen scattered through the walks, some of the old nuns walking sedately along, while others, more juvenile or gay, ran races, and swung each other in large ornamental swings placed in the grounds; while the girls who were being educated in the convent joined the games, and swelled the peals of laughter by their own gleeful mirth.

But it was the Reverend Mother who most impressed her, and no wonder!

She was tall and slight, long flowing black robes setting off the graceful outlines of her figure, and adding dignity to her movements; her features were long and regular, and her colour that peculiar creamy tint that is so still and delicate, yet far removed from denoting delicacy in its possessor; the straight white band across her forehead almost seemed to enhance the beauty of the well-shaped brow and delicately defined eyebrows that lay beneath it; but in her eyes and smile lay the fascination that made her irresistible. Usually the lids drooped over those lovely eyes, and the long black lashes literally rested on her cheeks: her mouth was perhaps a little too tightly closed; but what a change was visible in that apparently impassive face when the lips, parting in a smile, revealed the white, even rows of teeth within, and two lurking dimples near the corners of her mouth gave an almost magical sweetness to her expression! Then the raised eyelids gave to view the soft black velvet-like orbs, that seemed to enchain the

mine, took an acquaintance to see the Superior of the convent. Miss C—— walked with a young nun, a very sad-looking, but very pretty girl. Being rather interested in her she said, 'Are you not very happy here?' 'Happy! happy!' she exclaimed, with great feeling, 'I don't know the meaning of the word. But it won't be long. I shall soon be there,' pointing to the graveyard, 'or there,' pointing towards the lunatic asylum." This convent seems to have been conveniently situated.

gaze, and draw the beholder as by a hidden power or spell under their marvellous influence. Such was their effect on Emily as she addressed her.

Her remark, " Have you been long in this neighbourhood ? " seemed innocent enough, for Emily little knew that the question was merely asked to mislead her, and that her whole history and position were more intimately known to her questioner than by herself.

Moreover she began to view "the bright side of the picture through the new mental lens provided by" Mrs. Ellerby—" for so she was called by those not under her rule,"—and as days went on, "the cruel woman, by flattery of the most insinuating kind, obtained a powerful influence over Emily's mind."

So the weeks passed by. Emily visited the convent nearly every day : her letters from her aunt and Edward were intercepted. The priest was foiled in his final attempt to convert Emily, and retired discomfited :—

but, when he closed the door behind him, a malignant scowl crossed his face, and he shook his clenched hand in the direction of where he had left Emily standing, muttering as he did so : "I shall soon bring you to your senses, my lady, when I get you into my power ; " and, striding out of the house, he met Captain Seward, who had evidently been waiting for him.

Then was formulated the plot which was to cause such bitter suffering to our heroine.

That afternoon she went to the convent, and for the first time joined the sisterhood at Vespers. The T—— use seems to have been peculiar : here is its description :—

The Sisters entered in single file, each as she came in front of the altar prostrating herself, and then retiring to her place with downcast eyes, and hands meekly crossed upon her breast. When all the seats were filled, solemn silence reigned for a few minutes, and then the sweet voices of the sisterhood rose softly as they chanted a hymn to the Virgin. Had it been to the Lord, the great Giver of all goodness, how earnestly would Emily have joined in the strain; but the words of the hymn chilled all her devotional feelings. The sounds died away in a solemn cadence; and, prostrating themselves on the ground, the Sisters remained sunk in their devotions. Prayers over, a bell sounded through the passage, and, retiring as they had come, with a complete prostration before the altar, the sisterhood left the chapel.

And now, to quote the heading of this chapter, "The Plot Developed." Captain Seward sent to say he could not come for Emily, and she stayed the night in the convent,

utterly unconscious that she was delivered over to her soft-spoken gaoler as complete a captive as though the walls of Newgate enfolded her.

Next morning the Reverend Mother's amiability continued, and our heroine was taken to the garden by Sister Mary Raymond, "whose tall angular figure stood erect before Emily, as she seemed to look through her with her piercing light grey eyes." A "merry novice" invited Emily to swing, but she preferred to accompany Sister Mary Theresa, a tall, pale girl, with beautiful features and a deep sigh, to look at her flowers. She told Emily her history, which want of space compels me to omit; and shortly afterwards Mrs. Ellerby laid a hand on Emily's shoulder, saying, "You did not hear me approach."

If Emily had *seen* her approach she would have understood the reason why she could not have heard her, even though all her faculties had been on the alert. But she learnt before very long that in a convent every means is

studied by which a knowledge may be obtained of what is
going on in the hearts of its inmates; and the stealthy, cat-
like tread of the Reverend Mother, as she paced gravelled
walk and green sward alike with equal softness, taught her
that faces can be read at their pleasure by those who make
them their study, and who, stealing with velvet-shod foot-
steps upon the unwary dreamer, may learn in silence what
the tongue would never reveal.

Having received this instruction from Mrs. Ellerby's cat-like tread, Emily was allowed to see the
usual occupations of the Sisters, at such times as
services and swings did not engross their attention.

A number of the sisterhood were occupied in embroider-
ing robes for priests, and dressing up little figures of the
Virgin and St. Joseph. In a distant corner a group of
novices were busily engaged arranging the clothing on little
dolls, made to represent the Infant Christ, that they might
be laid in the Virgin's arms; while others were making
shrines of painted cardboard.

Recreation followed dinner. "Some of the nuns
were running races, others stood in a laughing group
round the swing;" but Emily looked round in vain for
Sister Mary Theresa.

Could she have visited the Superior's private room she
would have known the reason. Seated in her arm-chair, the
Reverend Mother looked severely on the pale girl who stood
meekly before her, apparently weighing how she should
address her, but in reality studying her face and drawing
her own conclusions. "Daughter," she at last said, "why
do you hold such conversations with one who is not yet one
of us? Is it wise?—is it kind?—is it just?"—"What do
you mean, my Mother?" asked the nun, with downcast
eyes.—" I ask you is it right of you to seek to prejudice one,
designed for a religious life, against its observances? If
your own vain thoughts and foolish imaginings have interrupted the happy course of your life with us, is it proper for
you to mislead one who may here find that happiness that

the world has failed to afford?"—"What have I done, my Mother?" again inquired the nun, as if mechanically.—"Daughter," said the Superior in a severe tone, "it is dangerous to play with edged tools. Beware in time; let me not warn you in vain; retire and repeat the Litany to the Virgin until Vespers."

Such, I grieve to say, was the prevailing laxity of the convent that these commands were not carried out; for Sister Mary Theresa, on reaching her cell, burst into tears:

a heavy stupor seemed to come over her, and the unhappy girl lay prone under its influence until the bell sounded for Vespers.

We regret that we cannot follow with Emily the ordinary routine of convent life—for, in accordance with a request from her father, our heroine remained an inmate of the convent. Another conversation with Sister Mary Theresa awakened her fears; hastily putting on her shawl and bonnet, she made her way to T——, where she found her father "seated with the priest at a table." Emily explained the misapprehension which had arisen in the convent, where they thought she wished to be a nun; but Captain Seward said that he was very busy, and Mr. Devine escorted her back.

The walk to the convent was a very silent one; and, as they entered Mrs. Ellerby's parlour, Emily, although naturally unsuspicious, could not help noticing the look of peculiar intelligence that was interchanged between the priest and the Superior.

A fortnight passed slowly by, and at last Emily determined to visit her father again, but at the gate the portress barred her egress. With "a flushed cheek and walking attire" she "entered the refectory, and advancing to Mrs. Ellerby, told her she wished to go into town." In answer, the Reverend Mother drew a letter with a Spanish postmark from her pocket and handed it silently to Emily, who read it and fainted. The letter ran thus :—

DAUGHTER,—On my arrival in England I found you a bigoted Protestant, and about to wed one as bigoted as yourself; and, having seen reason to join the only true Church, I could not leave my child to perish in a false one; therefore I brought you to T——, and have placed you in a position to learn to believe in a faith that will save your soul. You will see by the address that I write from a monastery in Spain. I am now dead to the world; and, having provided you with a place of safety for soul and body, I desire to forget all earthly ties and be nothing but the monk, brother Anselmo.

Your father,

H. SEWARD.

When Emily came to herself

she found that all her secular garments had been removed, and the robes and veil of a novice lay beside her bed.

She had hardly awoke

when the door opened gently, and the Superior and Sister Mary Raymond entered the room. "It is just as I thought," said the former; "the girl is like a foolish bird beating its wings against the bars of its cage. I begin to wish that Mr. Devine had chosen some other house for her."—"But remember the glory of converting a heretic, Reverend Mother," said Sister Mary Raymond; while her crafty, cold grey eyes rested unsympathizingly on the poor girl.—"Yes, you are right; I had forgotten that for the moment; but I fear we shall have some trouble in getting her to put on this dress," replied the Superior, pointing to it.—"Oh, that is easily managed; and once she has been seen in it by the sisterhood, she will not have any excuse for refusing to put it on again."—"But that is the very point that I do not know how to manage; I am sure she will not put it on of

her own free-will, and I do not like as yet to use force."—
"No force will be necessary; see, I shall prepare her for
it;" and drawing out a large cutting-out pair of scissors
from her pocket, Emily's shining ringlets were soon scattered
on the floor. "Now, while she is powerless to prevent it,
I shall, if you will assist me a little, put on the dress and
veil. You see," she said, after they had rapidly invested the
hapless girl in the garments she so much disliked, "it is
done; and now we must manage to have her seen by all
the Sisters." A quarter of an hour later Emily was roused
to consciousness by pungent aromatics; and, on looking
round her, found she was the centre of a pitying group as
she lay stretched on a sofa in the Superior's room, in dress
and appearance a nun.

Emily seems to have resigned herself to her fate,
comforted by the fact that she retained her Bible,
which was in a pocket of her underclothing and so
escaped notice, although its bulk must have been considerable.

An interlude styled "The Jesuit in Disguise" has
nothing to do with the story: we must also pass by
"A Profession and a Miracle," and come to the time
when, after a year, it was necessary for Emily to take
the final vows.

Her precious little Bible had as yet escaped detection,
and from its Divine teaching she had received strength and
help in many a time of trial. Various and severe were the
penances she had been forced to undergo for repeated
refusals to confess to the priest, after she had withstood all
the blandishments used by Mrs. Ellerby to induce her to
do so. And now a fresh trial awaited her; for the Bishop
was expected within the week to invest her with the black
veil, and receive her formal vows. It was in vain for Emily
to declare that willingly she never would pronounce them;
the preparations for the ceremony were continued, quite
regardless of her protestations; and when the important
day arrived, she was summoned to the Superior's room, to
receive her directions before proceeding to the chapel.

Nuns and Convents.   13

Having heard them in silence, Emily once more, in the most solemn manner, assured her that she would not take the vows binding herself to a life-long imprisonment, uncongenial to her mind, and to a religion that she could not profess. As usual the Superior heard her calmly to the end, thus gaining full evidence of what was in her mind without betraying by look or manner how it affected her; and without any comment she walked to a table on which was placed a tray with refreshments, and pouring out a glass of wine, she handed it to Emily, saying: "Drink that, you will require some support in the scene through which you are about to pass." Grateful for this show of kindness, and feeling her need of even artificial strength, Emily drank the wine; but in a few moments a dreamy languor came over her, and when she was summoned to the chapel, she followed the Superior mechanically, apparently without a will or wish of her own, and quite passive in her hands. The ceremony commenced immediately; and in the same slow, measured manner Emily went through it, seemingly utterly unconscious of what was going on, repeating the responses as she was ordered; and to the surprise of every one (except those in the secret), apparently quite without emotion of any kind. After the ceremony she retired to her cell, and overcome by irrepressible drowsiness, sank into a profound slumber that lasted till the bell for supper sounded through the house.

A conversation of some length with Sister Mary Theresa on the way to the refectory opened Emily's eyes.

Sister Mary Theresa was right in her conjectures. *The wine had been drugged.*[1] Seeing Emily's determined manner, the Superior felt assured she would refuse to take the vows, and in order to avoid a scene that might create a scandal in her convent, and also determined to bring Emily entirely within the power of the Church, she had infused a strong narcotic in the wine, and under its growing influence, Emily had acted mechanically as she was desired.

---

[1] Here, as throughout the quotations, the italics are those of the original.

Once in their power, Emily's life was made a burden to her. She refused to give up her Bible, and instead of taking it away from her, as most folk would have done,[1] the Reverend Mother made her walk on her knees up and down the gravel walk. Emily had hidden the Bible in a safe place, but Sister Mary Theresa, not being restricted in her locomotion, sped away and found it untouched.

Hiding it in her robe, she hastened from the spot, and avoiding Emily, joined the party at the swing, with an appearance of gaiety that was assumed for the purpose of misleading any one who might observe her. As the Sisters entered the chapel for Vespers, she contrived to pass close to Emily, and slipped the little volume into her hand; Emily as speedily concealing it in her wide sleeve, while she gave her friend a look of unutterable gratitude. From this

---

[1] Nothing is more striking in these stories than the ease with which the Papists are baffled. A pamphlet entitled *Monasticism Unveiled: Part II. The Climax* (Kensit), consists for the most part of " appalling revelations made by the escaped inmate of an English convent, less than three years ago " [1886]. Many of the revelations are even more disgusting than they are ludicrous; but in the following extract the latter quality predominates. " One day my mother, in a fit of anger, told me I must go straight to hell when I died, *as I had never been baptized*. After a time she wanted me to be baptized, for she said God was withholding His blessing from her for not having had her children baptized. (This mother was a nun.) 'And were you baptized?' 'No!' she said indignantly, 'I would not be forced into it.' 'And what did your mother do?' 'She appealed to a priest who was standing by, and he said: "Starve her till she does!" So I was starved for a fortnight, *down in the dungeons where so many are starved to death!* The only friend I had in the convent came once or twice, when she had an opportunity, and put in *a cup of water between* the bars!' (This was the friend who met her death for befriending her by loosening the tight binding which interfered with the action of her heart and lungs.) 'And how did you escape?' 'At the end of a fortnight my mother went to another convent, and my friend came and let me out, saying that she would take the responsibility on herself.' " I hardly expect to be believed when I say that the ostensible author of this pamphlet was no less a person than the late General Sir Robert Phayre, G.C.B.!

time she never ventured to remove it from her person during the day, and at night it lay securely under her head.

But it must be confessed she had a bad time of it.

Many were the persecutions she underwent from the Superior and her assistant, Sister Mary Raymond, when they discovered how useless it was to combat her religious belief, or to force upon her the acceptance of their own. The most menial offices in the household, as well as the most laborious, were assigned her; and although her health and spirit gave way under this cruel tyranny, her courage remained undaunted. Among other penances, was one that was very distasteful to her. It was this: at certain hours the pupils passed through a long hall on their way to the playground, or to dinner or supper; and at those hours she was obliged either to walk on her knees up and down the hall, or to kneel there without support while the girls went by. At other times she was ordered to wash the hall; and Sister Mary Raymond stood over her finding fault, and making her go over parts of her work again, in order to humiliate her before the pupils.

But worse was to follow. Like a true missionary Emily preached to such nuns as she could influence—and it is wonderful how many opportunities she seems to have enjoyed—and especially to Sister Mary Theresa, who at last made up her mind that she would read the Bible, and that no man should prevent her. But she reckoned without Sister Mary Raymond, who said,

stepping from behind the pillar, "The Reverend Mother shall know of this. Go to your cell; it is advancing towards morning;" and motioning to the terrified girls to walk before her, the stern old nun marched them to their cells.

Sister Mary Raymond was as good as her word.

As Emily left her cell the next morning, she presented herself, with compressed lips and frowning brow, and prevented her egress. "Return to your cell, wretched girl," said she harshly; "the Reverend Mother will deal with you when the morning duties are over." With a shudder, Emily re-entered the room, and heard a bolt shot to on the outside of the door before the solemn tread of Sister Mary Raymond's feet moved from it.

When the Reverend Mother arrived on the scene, she snatched Emily's Bible from her hand, and "consigned it to a pocket concealed in her dress." She then told Emily to follow her, "down a flight of stairs hidden from general view by a door." This is not unusual with cellar stairs.

At length the Reverend Mother stopped at a low door in the underground part of the house; and, having a kind of idea that it was a coal vault, or some such place, Emily followed her into it. A dim light was burning in the vault; but before Emily had time to distinguish any object, she heard the key turn in the lock, and, rushing to the door, found it securely fastened on the outside. She was alone and a prisoner. In her horror at her position, Emily looked wildly around, seeking for some means of escape; but there was neither window nor door, except the one by which she had entered. The dim light now revealed to her a low, vaulted room, entirely built of stone; in one corner was a truckle bedstead with a mattress; a chair and table being the only other furniture in the room. Once more Emily rushed to the door, and almost phrenzied by terror, beat her hands wildly against it; but the hard iron only bruised and hurt her, without conveying a sound to the outside world.

Here she remained; meanwhile other matters were taking place which demand attention.

Unknown to the Superior, an undercurrent of rebellion against her authority had been for some time prevailing in the convent; and, as it was countenanced by the confessor, a Mr. Shelden, it had gained strength and form before she was even aware of its existence; and, curious to say, the very effort she made to assert her complete authority over the wills and persons of the sisterhood was the immediate means of determining the more daring spirits engaged in the conspiracy to act for themselves, and openly set her at defiance.

The ringleader of this rebellion was Sister Mary Catherine,

an elderly nun, whose round face and merry eyes spoke more for a love of fun and good living than for her enjoyment of conventual discipline. This nun was rather a notability in the convent, as she was possessed of property settled on her in such a manner that she alone could draw its revenues, which could not be alienated to the convent without her consent, and in case of her death she could will it to whom she pleased. Her position had been always a very pleasant one, as she had the power of leaving her money outside the convent walls had she chosen; therefore quarter-day was always a gala-day with her, and, as she had always been very munificent in her gifts, the Superior had no cause of complaint against her, except the secret feeling of envy of her independence, which she could not always repress, and which sometimes exhibited itself in petty annoyances and impositions of penance very galling to such a mind as that of Sister Mary Catherine, who did not at all admire fasting or being deprived of a favourite dish, especially when it was placed temptingly within her reach.

Aided by Mr. Shelden, the rebellion had attained considerable importance, and Sister Mary Theresa having overheard a whispered conference between the confessor and Sister Mary Catherine, her participation in the proposed flight was made the price of her silence.

That night, Sister Mary Theresa sat in her cell, anxiously awaiting a tap at the door. It came—

and gently turning the handle she passed into the gallery, and sped swiftly down the stairs, and through the side door into the garden, where several dark figures were already standing clustered together. "Are we all here?" asked Sister Mary Catherine, in a whisper.—"Yes, Reverend

Mother," replied a voice, in an equally low tone. With a gratified thrill, as the title fell on her ears, the new Superior turned towards the gate, where Mr. Shelden stood waiting for them; and in a minute more the entire party were on the road, and free as the air they breathed. . . . Two carriages were in waiting at a little distance; and putting the nuns into them, the priest mounted the box of the first, and directed the coachman to drive to a house in the town where he had already engaged lodgings for the nuns, and in the drawing-room of which they were soon seated round a table, on which stood a goodly supper ordered by the provident forethought of the Superior, who presided in the most hospitable manner. The blazing fire, brilliant lights and goodly fare, with the hilarity of the new Superior, and the attentive care of her satellite the confessor, were all equally new and bewildering to the released nuns, who could hardly believe their senses at the wonderful transformation.

The escape of the nuns caused some commotion at St. Mary's Convent, and

the Bishop was immediately appealed to; but, being convinced by the *weighty* arguments of Sister Mary Catherine, that the sum of £90,000 at her disposal would be lost to the Church for ever, if her arrangements were interfered with, he very wisely left her to her own devices, and admonished the Superior to be more careful in future to keep watch and ward over her charge; thus giving her a double wound—in her authority and guardianship.

Things were worse than ever in the convent, "for, in her anger at the escape of the few, the Superior exhausted her ingenuity in tormenting the many." Emily especially had much to put up with.

In the meantime, the liberated party at T—— contrived to make the time pass very pleasantly. Curiously enough, the priest had selected the house of a Protestant widow in which to locate the nuns; and, much to the astonishment of the worthy woman, their conduct did not much agree with her preconceived ideas of convent discipline. Before

Nuns and Convents. 19

Lent commenced the day was one round of enjoyment, which consisted chiefly in ordering and partaking of every good thing that the season afforded, with a little interlude of novel-reading, or other amusements, to get over the time. Lent, however, changed the scene a little, but if for the better, the good woman could not decide. Since she had taken up her abode at Mrs. Carter's, the new Superior had provided herself with a worldly dress, also one that would fit any figure, in which each of the nuns were habited in their turn. Every morning, taking one of the sisters as her companion, the Superior set out to market and shop; and the quantity of good things she sent in bewildered the worthy Mrs. Carter, who thought it almost impossible that they could all be used. As Lent commenced of course the order of things was a little changed; but the description of one day will suffice for all. According to convent rule, a slight refreshment in the morning, followed by dinner at noon, and a refection (as it is called) at night, are the full allowance of meals; and, determined to keep to the letter of the rule, the Superior contrived to manage very well in her own observance of it. Rising at a very late hour, the "slight refreshment," consisting of tea and toast, was found to be amply sufficient until dinner-time at noon; when a long table, extending through the room, one end of which was laid for dinner, while the other had all the appliances for tea, by the simple expedient of remaining at the table from the time dinner commenced until it was time for tea, the entire performance was made to represent one meal; after which the table was taken away, and fun, frolic, and dancing, in which Mr. Shelden joined, were the order of the night—the "refection" being a nice substitute for supper before the party broke up. Dismembered chairs and broken footstools bore record to the liveliness of the party, to the great scandal of the sober landlady, who was perfectly horrified at such proceedings, so much opposed to all her preconceived ideas of convent life; but the gay Superior and her merry nuns laughed at her scruples, and amused themselves while they could, only too glad to have the opportunity, and determined to avail themselves of it to the fullest extent.

Mr. Shelden was the life and soul of the party, after the Superior; and many a game of "Blindman's Buff" and

"Puss in the Corner" gave evidence of his enjoyment of the fun; his only drawback being an ever-present fear that the Bishop might hear that the proceedings of the new sisterhood were not exactly as strict as they might be, and issue some veto accordingly; but Lent drew to a close, and the life and gaiety of the party were undisturbed by any interference on the part of his diocesan, and, as time passed, the priest became more at ease; and at length the entire party seemed to have formed themselves into a committee of pleasure, not very unlike the Decameronian scenes described by Boccaccio, and which at last produced a determined order from Mrs. Carter to quit her house, several milder intimations of her desire for peaceable possession having failed to produce any effect.

Sister Mary Theresa had always demurred to the Decameronian scenes, in which she found "a new and extremely unpleasant element;" so she consulted Mrs. Carter, who introduced her to the curate. Who should this be but Edward Stanley, the *fiancé* of Emily! A fortunate accident led to this discovery: it was followed up, with the result that the sad history of Emily was revealed. Having flown from one convent, it was easy to escape from another: Mr. Stanley came in a carriage and took Sister Mary Theresa away.

There was a hurried rush upstairs, an opening and shutting of doors, and various exclamations of surprise and alarm. Some of the nuns had seen Sister Mary Theresa enter the carriage with a gentleman, and as it was driven from the door they hastened to tell the news to the Superior, who was enjoying a little repose in her own room, and who at first could scarcely believe it possible that one of her pets could break away from her good-natured rule; but comforting herself with the reflection that, if the runaway was not content, it was much better to let her depart, she settled herself more comfortably in her easy chair, and was soon enjoying again the quiet repose that had been interrupted by such strange news.

Nuns and Convents. 21

Accompanied by Mr. Delmore, a magistrate, and by Mrs. Stanley, they drove to St. Mary's, where they were received by Mrs. Ellerby with much courtesy. But, when they asked for Miss Seward,

had a shell exploded beside her, the blank consternation of a Superior could not have been greater; she sat with distended eyes and colourless face, staring vacantly before her.

This aroused the suspicions of her visitors, and when she denied that Emily was on the premises, Mr. Delmore said:—

"Madame, I must inform you that you have placed yourself in the power of the law, by detaining Miss Seward here contrary to her will; I am a magistrate, and I have provided Mr. Stanley with a search-warrant, therefore I must insist that you at once lead us to Miss Seward's room, otherwise I shall proceed immediately to search the house for her. You have now your choice; and I warn you, for your own sake, not to give us any further trouble, or to try to resist my authority."—"*Miss Seward* is not here, as I told you," said Mrs. Ellerby, craftily sheltering her falsehood under a subterfuge; "she who was Miss Seward in the world, is now Sister Mary Angela in Religion; and your authority does not extend to a professed nun, who has taken the vows."—"You are mistaken, madam," said the magistrate coolly; "my authority enables me to liberate every nun in your convent, if they are disposed to leave it, even though their vows were voluntary; but," he added significantly, "we are well aware of the mode by which you secured Miss Seward's apparent acquiescence in the pretended profession you compelled her to make."

The Reverend Mother was in a tight place.

Biting her lips with baffled rage, she turned to the door and left the room, followed closely by the magistrate, Mrs. Stanley, and Edward. Turning quickly into a side passage, she hastened down the stairs leading to the lower part of the house, and taking a key from her pocket, she hissed from between her teeth, "Take her, if you like, but you will not have her very long;" and, flinging open the door of the vault, she turned from them and walked rapidly away. For a moment the dim light prevented their distinguishing any object in the vault; but, as their eyes became more accustomed to it, they saw the miserable bed, and on it the attenuated figure of Emily in her nun's garb.

Emily "tried to fling herself into the extended arms of Edward and her aunt," but in this she not unnaturally failed, and "sank back in a state of helpless weakness." But they got her into the carriage, and she "was soon on her way to her aunt's house, her head pillowed on the heart that beat so truly for her," *i.e.*, Edward's.

Mr. Delmore stopped to have it out with Mrs. Ellerby, who met him "with a sullen brow and fiery eyes." He insisted on having Emily's Bible.

Almost suffocated with suppressed fury, the Superior turned to her desk, and, taking out the little Bible, threw it contemptuously on the table, exclaiming, "There, sir, take your wonderful prize, and now rid me of your presence."—"Be assured that I do so with the greatest pleasure," replied Mr. Delmore, as he placed the book in his pocket. "I never thought it would be my misfortune to come in contact with a woman like you, deprived of all the attributes that make her lovely and attractive, a moral deformity far beyond any physical defects; but, take one warning, that if your wickedness should prove to have any lasting effect on Miss Seward, you shall not escape unpunished. I shall make it my own business to see justice done upon you;" and, so saying, the magistrate left the house, without another glance at the wicked woman, who, terrified at last, lest she really might be made amenable to the laws she had violated, sat down immediately and wrote to the Bishop to try to negotiate for her removal to another convent.

She was removed, and Sister Mary Catherine,

Nuns and Convents. 23

having previously endowed the convent with her large fortune, was duly installed in her place.

Her return with her small company was hailed with joy by the sisterhood, who looked forward to a new state of things under her light, easy rule; but when did the Church of Rome keep faith when it was politic to do otherwise? Having secured her person and her fortune, it had no further need of Sister Mary Catherine; and, to her horror and amazement, as well as to the grief of the sisterhood, the poor lady was ordered to return to her former position in the convent, with a warning to conduct herself well, or her irregularities, while absent in the town, would be severely inquired into and punished. A French Superior, from a very strict convent, was placed over the sisterhood; and fasting and penance once more mortified the community of St. Mary.

We are not told what became of Mr. Shelden. Captain Seward remained in the Order of St. Joseph; Edward and Emily were married; Sister Mary Theresa and Mr. Delmore followed their example.

Thus "out of evil came good;" and in after years, at many a Christmas gathering, the friends recounted scenes from their past experience to illustrate the evils of convent life.

I have dealt with this story at considerable length, because it contains the stock features which characterize Protestant stories, and is, moreover, entirely free from the indecencies which often render convent fictions unsuitable for general perusal. It is difficult to imagine that it is written seriously, especially when it is remembered that the scene is laid in Ireland, where one would have thought the proceedings of the escaped nuns at T—— would have attracted attention. It will be seen that the nuns went to the Offices with much regularity, but Mass does not seem to have been said in the convent, and indeed the only time we hear of it all through the story is at night, "with incense and requiems," in the Spanish monastery. One remarkable feature is the absence of motive for the detention and ill-treatment of Emily. This inconsequence is characteristic of these stories, and attained its height in the veracious narrative of Miss Golding[1]—who was bringing in by her accomplishments a thousand a year to her convent, and yet the nuns tried to murder her!

Another point worthy of notice is the comparative cheerfulness of the community at St. Mary's. Running races, gardening, and swinging, formed part of their ordinary pursuits. Nor was there any difficulty in inspecting the convent: Mr. Delmore had merely to state that he was a magistrate, and the Reverend Mother responded, "If you compel me, I must obey," and led the way to Emily's cell.

But my aim in this chapter is to show what is said by Protestants about convents, not to comment on it. So I will pass on to *The Sisters of Seville: a Convent Story*, by A. L. M. This is one of "Horner's Penny Stories," and is now in its 175th thousand.

Clara and Inez de Valdes had been brought up in a convent near Seville.

The girls had been struck by Mother Agneta being absent from Mass, and one day, when alone with her in the novices' apartment, Clara asked, "Do you never go to Mass, Mother?"

"No, my child. I have rested my soul on the one ce for sin, the Lord Christ, and I know no other; s is nothing but an idol made by men."

Ellen Golding, the Rescued Nun. By the Rev. S. F. Smith, S., 1d.

Nuns and Convents.

Now Mother Agneta was the mistress of the novices. Why Clara and Inez, who were to return to the world, were in "the novices' apartment" does not appear: but it is even more remarkable that prolonged absence from Mass on the part of the novice-mistress seems to have passed unnoticed. Mother Agneta promptly proceeded to tell the girls her story. A little muleteer gave her the Gospel of St. John, from which she discovered she was a sinner. She thereupon inflicted severe penances upon herself—some of which, such as lying on ashes, must, one would have thought, have attracted the attention of the convent authorities—and finally told Father Luiz, who "urged confession." Agneta, however, having discovered that "no earthly priest had power to forgive sins," declined; but "one night after Compline" she opened the Testament, and found the words, "Thy faith hath saved thee." This convinced her that "neither priests nor saints nor penances saved the soul," and she became happy.

Shortly afterwards she became sick unto death.

Her breath came in short gasps, and the cold dew was already on her forehead, as the door of the cell opened, and the Abbess entered, accompanied by a monk bearing the Host.

"Peace be to thee, Mother Agneta," he said, as he drew near the pallet; but as his eyes fell on the nun, he said quickly, "She is dying and has not confessed. Sister, in what faith do you die?"

A look so radiant spread over the pale face and lit up the glazing eyes, that the Abbess and monk stood silent. The dying woman raised herself with a great effort, and said in a whisper: "Christ only! No Mass, no Sacrament, no priest. He saves, He alone. Jesus, I come!"

"Mother Agneta, what are you saying? I cannot absolve you in such deadly heresy. Alas! you are wandering, perchance from pain or weakness of body. Look, and confess your sins," and he held the crucifix before her.[1]

"'Tis an idol, take it away," gasped the nun. "The Blood of Jesus is all my plea, on that rests my soul. See," and her eyes were fixed with an unearthly look on one corner of the room, "He comes!"

There was a slight sigh, and Mother Agneta was with the Lord.

One can hardly wonder that Father Luiz exclaimed, "A pretty state of things! and the Mother of the Novices to boot!" On finding that the two De Valdeses had "tended her," he remarked :—

"It will be well to have them both to confession before they leave; and one, if not both, must enter the convent in another year; we cannot afford to lose a dowry like theirs. As for her, she must be buried in the strangers' part of our cemetery. I will allow no heretic among the faithful."

The new Mother of the Novices, a harsh, bigoted woman, whose name was Mother Beatriz, bewailed it with many crossings to Inez de Valdes.

"Ay de mi, my daughter, this is terrible, and she we thought a saint! Who can tell where the wicked one enters? I never thought he would take possession of Mother Agneta. And you, my children, too, have been with her. Our Lady grant ye have learnt none of her doctrines. She will be buried without any rites of the Church; she is a lost soul."

"Nay, Mother Beatriz, once a saint she is one now. I would I were as safe," said Inez.

"This must to the Abbess, daughter, and she will deal with you," said the Mother. "You have been learning of her heresy."

"I have learnt that the Lord Jesus is the only Saviour from sin," replied Inez.

"Go to your cell, foolish girl! I trust it is only an

---

[1] I am inclined to think that the author considers "the Host" and the "crucifix" synonymous; this view is supported by the accompanying picture, in which the crucifix alone is represented.

idea; you must see no one till the Holy Mother has learnt it."

We cannot follow the sisters through their course, which ended, as might have been expected, at the stake; for our business is with nuns, and although this is called "a convent story," there is nothing more about convents in it. And a word must be said in praise of the illustrations with which it abounds: there is one of the Archbishop of Toledo, making an afternoon call in full pontificals, which speaks well for the imagination of the artist. The Archbishop, by the way, was the brother of Mother Agneta, whose views he shared.

Priest and Nun: a Story of Convent Life, is a bulky volume of 476 pages, by Mrs. Julia McNair Wright (Hodder & Stoughton). It is "an attempt to give a true picture of the inner life of the modern nunnery" as it exists in the United States; and, like most of its class, is "strictly based on facts: no statement is made that cannot be justified by actual history." The most interesting inmate of the convent is Sister Clement, whom we first meet in her disguise of a maid-servant.

Annette was evidently of French origin. Her hair was drawn back from her face, the ends curling, her cap was ornamented with pink ribbons, her teeth might be false, her cheeks were undeniably rouged. Her mistress pronounced her an admirable servant.

But when her domestic duties were over she returned to the convent and

cast away her serving-maid finery, took off her high-heeled boots, and grew shorter; removed her black wig and pink cap, and lo! thin, light hair; washed away the rouge and pearl powder, and there was a haggard, yellow face, with whitish eyebrows. Next she clad herself in the dress of her Order. . . . She was no longer Annette, she was Sister Clement—a staid, thin, bent nun of about forty.

Sister Clement then went to the Oratory of " the House Without a Name," and there told the Reverend Mother—an excitable person, Ignatia by name, who continually " beat her breast with her long bony hands "—the conversations she had heard while waiting at table. Ignatia, who had given herself and her money to the Order of Jesuits, had with her " only those sworn to the most rigid Jesuitical severities ; " but her director, Father Murphy, although not an attractive person, did his best to bring her to reason. He went to the chapel, where she " kept her bootless vigils." "'Rise up, daughter Ignatia!' he said grandly ; " and when she asked him to exorcise her he ordered soup and bread. "'I am sworn to fasting,' faltered Ignatia. 'I release you,' said Father Murphy, 'and do not swear yourself to that again for a month.'" He then administered an opiate, after which Ignatia insisted upon going to confession. Having accused herself of "the nine ways of being accessory to others' sins, of the seven deadly sins, and of five sins against the Holy Ghost," she was proceeding to "the four sins crying to Heaven for vengeance," when Father Murphy interrupted her, pointing out that she had confessed these sins full nineteen times, and had received absolution. " If I have not benefited you by nineteen absolutions, what can you hope from the twentieth ? " demanded Father Murphy practically. But he gave her absolution all the same.

" Vast the difference between Mother Ignatia and

Mother Robart," who presided over the Convent of the Immaculate Heart. " She wore the usual dress of an Abbess, which became her well; but she was a Sybarite in Holy Orders. Her dress was of the richest and softest material ; costly her rosary; costly her crucifix ; costly and dainty every item from her head-gear to her silken hose and kid shoes."[1] In her convent the nuns were called " Saint " or " Sister " indifferently; they also spelt indifferently, judging from the fact that one of them is always styled " Cecelia."[2] A number of Protestant girls went to the school, which seems to have been a good one, and several " had been privately received into full com-

---

[1] The descriptions of the dress worn by the nuns of Protestant fiction are delightfully various. In a Spanish convent, for example, the novices wore "the habit of the novitiate, and a banner adorned with flowers" (*English Churchman*, 20th January, 1898, p. 39)—surely a singularly inconvenient form of vestment. In this convent " the veil lasts for life," and must therefore be made of an excellent wearing material.

[2] " Sister Cecelia had one crowning merit—she wrote a most beautiful hand. She formed English, French, and German script like the fairest specimens of copper-plate. Before her humble girlhood two paths of life had opened—to be a writing-mistress in schools and private families, or to bring herself and her talent into the convent. Deciding to take vows and the veil, she at once became a *saint*. Oh, short and broad and easy road to Heaven—a garb, a promise, a fixed routine of living ; and lo ! a portal, said of salvation, opened wide. . . . As in duty bound, when at so little sacrifice of her loneliness and poverty Sister Cecelia had from the Church at once her daily living and her saintship, she served that Church with ardour. We can give no better definition of this nun than that we find in *The Constitutions and Declarations of the Jesuits*, published in France in 1762. ' One ought to permit himself to be conducted and directed as if a corpse, which is moved as any one wills ; or as the cane in an old man's hand, which serves any end for which the owner employs it, and upon whatever side he chooses to turn it.' Sister Cecelia lived, moved, wrote (copies), spoke, thought, for the Church. Her even, gliding step, her cold, steady eye, her monotone running in set form, ' My dear child, thus and so,' as clear, as even, and as unexpressive as endless repetitions of E flat in the treble, with never another note struck between, were all the outward tokens of her passive, unreasoning, unstirred inner life."

munion with the Church of Rome, their parents being in blissful ignorance of the fact." Mother Robart had an eagle eye, as well as a nephew who, "while unfortunately lacking all religious feelings, was certainly not a Romanist:" and the eagle eye detected the nephew when he visited the convent, talking to one of the Protestant pupils, who had just observed to him: "The convent is a prison, and I can hear the clank of the chains under all the flowers and finery." Agnes was sent next day to the House Without a Name. "The main object of this House Without a Name," which was always approached by a circuitous route, "was to have it a perfectly secret place, unknown to almost every one, where difficult cases might be quietly handled." Agnes soon found that this was a much less pleasant place to stay in than the Convent of the Immaculate Heart, in which "Friday's fast brought fish, eggs, buttered toast, fruit, and cream, and confections. In the House Without a Name, they had a small allowance of bread and water after Matins, and nothing more until after Vespers, when they had water gruel and a crust of brown bread. In all these rigours Agnes must take part."

Meanwhile Sister Clement was instructing Sister Maria how to take a situation as nursemaid. She herself had been very successful in baptizing Protestant children, and instructed Sister Maria how to do it, adding: "I generally sign the Cross on the child and say an *Ave* at each point." Sister Clement subsequently became maid to a Protestant girl, but was recalled to the convent by a letter to say that her mother was dying.

An hour after Annette started "to see her dying mother," she was, to all outward appearance, hanging on the wall of an upper room in the House Without a Name, and Sister Clement was busy over embroidery and "exercises." Lilly would never have recognized Sister Clement as Annette; but she would doubtless have been amazed to see Annette's hair, bonnet, and set of false teeth suspended on the otherwise bare wall of a nun's cell.

I cannot now devote further space to this remarkable book, but I shall have to refer to it again when priests come under review. Sister Clement continues her evil course to the very end of the volume. We last find her taking care of a prisoner concealed on the fourth storey of the House Without a Name, for whom she invented a new and terrible torture: she "hung up in her room horrid pictures of fictitious saints and martyrs." It may be that this Nameless House is the head-quarters of the "horrid" religious pictures which still abound in our midst. This "fourth storey" presents certain difficulties, for we were distinctly told that the House Without a Name was "a three-storey house." But students of Johnson's *Dictionary* will find a similar contradiction in the definitions: "*Garret*, the topmost room of a house; *Cock-loft*, the room above the garret."

A perusal of these evident absurdities—mere samples of what might be adduced—suggests reflections so obvious that it is unnecessary to set them forth. It cannot fail to be remarked that this class of Protestant fiction, which has been more or less in evidence at least since the beginning of the century, has proved absolutely powerless to arrest the steady growth among us of the very institutions against which it is directed. Protestants themselves see this clearly enough, and record that whereas in 1829 England had 16 convents and no monasteries, we had in 1895 491 convents and 244 monasteries; and the number is steadily increasing.[1] Besides these, there are a large number of Anglican convents, showing that the benefits and attractions of the conventual system are realized by those outside the Church. We may regret that such nonsense as these stories contain should be disseminated so widely, and that a certain number of our otherwise sensible countrymen and countrywomen should still be deluded by it. But we may console ourselves by the manifest fact that this number is diminishing, and that the growing influence of the Church in our midst is accompanied by the increasing weakness of her enemies.

[1] *The Protestant Woman*, October, 1895, p. 12.

II. JESUITS.

I HAD in the first instance intended to treat Jesuits and priests in the same chapter, and no one acquainted with Protestant fiction would wonder if I had done so. So far from having extended the term Jesuit beyond its popular meaning, I should have restricted it, for the honour of belonging to the Society of Jesus is frequently attributed by Protestants not only to all priests, but also to the Catholic laity.[1] Nor is it only ignorant Protestants who hold this opinion. A well-known Catholic barrister was once written to by a still more widely known journalist, for some information regarding the Jesuits, "to which body," said he, "I believe that you belong"; and I remember how, during my first walk with the late Lord Tennyson, he suddenly turned to me and said, "Are you a Jesuit?" and when I said, "No," rejoined, "Well, you *are* a Roman Catholic," as though the two were, at any rate to some extent, synonymous. This is also the view of the Church Association as represented by Mr. Wm. Allen, Captain of the "Protestant Van *Earl of Shaftesbury*," who in his report for 1892 [2] writes as follows:—

WOLVEY.—Squire Arnold was once a Ritualistic priest in the Church of England, and since he became a Romanist he has built a chapel. In a very short time they have

---

[1] It is only fair, however, to say that the distinction between Jesuits and Catholics is clearly perceived by some writers. Thus Charles Kingsley tells us that the defects of Eustace Leigh's character "came upon [him], not because he was a Romanist, but because he was educated by the Jesuits, . . . and the Upas-shadow which has blighted the whole Romish Church blighted him also" (*Westward Ho*, ch. iii.).

[2] *Our Colporteurs.* No. IV. Church Association.

succeeded in drawing about forty Protestants into the Popish net. The Jesuit visits the village daily, walks through the shops, houses, etc., and has succeeded in making friends with the people. He carries sweets for the children, and taps them on the cheeks. He also carries tobacco for the young fellows, and he doesn't mind visiting their club; and on some occasions he has written to the club asking them to attend the chapel to hear him preach. When the Squire gets the chance of a house occupied by a Protestant, he buys it out and hands it over to a Romanist. A coal man got an old horse bought him for going over, and the landlord's wife at the Blue Pig has gone over; the Jesuit buys butter and eggs from her. Some of the shopkeepers were afraid to open their doors while my van stood in the streets, and they were all forbidden to come near this heretic during his stay at Wolvey.

The charm of this account would be marred by comment, yet for my purpose it is necessary to explain that the Rev. Austin Richardson, who was then priest at Wolvey, was not a member of the Society of Jesus. The honours of Protestant distinction certainly rest with the Jesuits—" the most poisonous microbes ever introduced into the Church "—" one of the most mischievous organizations that ever disturbed the peace and happiness of mankind," to quote the chairman of a recent National Protestant Congress.

One of their most striking characteristics is their fondness for disguises. These are of various kinds: the female Jesuit affects the domestic *rôle* of governess, nurse, or housemaid;[1] the male Jesuit often poses as

[1] Here is an instance from *The Protestant Woman* for August, 1897:—" M——, my medical maid, once came across a Jesuit. A woman came into a house where M. was then living as a housemaid. She pretended to be very illiterate—unable, in fact, to read or write. The family being thus thrown off their guard, left letters and papers about which enabled her to gain the information she required. M. can't quite remember the incidents of her leaving; it was in an unpleasant way, but to every one's astonishment, she wrote out a full receipt for wages in a thoroughly well-educated hand."

a clergyman of the Church of England.[1] He has been doing this for a long while, and has been exposed so often that one wonders he can ever be successful.

"It is a fact which no one who knows anything of the state of things in this country can question, that we are swarming with Jesuits;" and "the success which the agents of Rome have met with in our Church has been such as to increase largely the danger arising from the operations of her direct and commissioned emissaries."[2] This is set forth with much detail in an anonymous pamphlet entitled, *The Jesuits. What are they? Who are they? What have they done? What are they doing?*[3] A clergyman of the Established Church, the Rev. F. A. C. Lillingston, contributes a wonderful preface, of which I have only space to quote the opening sentence.

As I am sure that we are living in very dangerous times, and that if we are not walking very close to Christ we shall easily be led away from the faith once delivered to the saints, I hail with unfeigned delight any publication whose object is to open our eyes to the fearful iniquities of the Romish system, and the snake-like character of the Jesuit system.

After the usual profuse expenditure of adjectives, and a number of interesting statements which fully entitle this pamphlet to a place under the head of Protestant Fiction—*e.g.* that, "persuaded by the

---

[1] Sometimes, however, he pretends to belong to a religious order other than his own: "the Padre Guiliamo [*sic*] was a monk of one of the Dominican orders—at least he gave himself out as such, though he was, in fact, a Jesuit." *Jessie's Bible, or the Italian Priest*, by Mrs. S. Kelly, p. 3 (Book Society: no date).

[2] *Rome's Tactics*. By the Very Rev. William Goode, D.D. Forty-second thousand. London: Nisbet, 1893.

[3] Banks & Son, Racquet Court, London. 1d.

Jesuits, Archbishop Manning drew up a petition in favour" of the definition of Papal Infallibility—we come to "The Jesuit Plot to betray the Church of England." The information given under this head supplies incidentally many details of Cardinal Newman's career which have been unaccountably overlooked by his biographers, and should not be lost sight of when his life comes to be written. Here are one or two sentences :—

> The preceding parts of this tract have been written in a moderate tone [1]—as no cause is enhanced by fiery language—and will show that the Jesuits can, for purposes of their own, stoop to any enormity that it is possible to conceive; that they are capable of every crime; and their expulsion from every country, and even suppression by a Pope, clearly demonstrates this. There can, therefore, be little doubt that the Romeward movement in the Church of England is the work of the Jesuits. It has been suggested that Dr. Pusey himself belonged to the "Fifth Order." . . . It must be remembered that Dr. Newman spent the early years of his life in the College of the *Propaganda Fide* at Rome, and there can be no doubt that he was a Romanist then. The fact is, he was a Papist while ministering in the pale of the Reformed Church of England.
>
> "The progress of Roman Catholicism in this country within the last thirty years," declares one writer, "is almost incredible. . . . For this increase Romanism is indebted to members of the Society of Jesus, and especially to those members of that Order who officiate as clergymen in the Established Church of this land." An eminent prelate

---

[1] *E.g.* "The infernal pile" (p. 8); "the sinister and diabolical smile of the Jesuits" (p. 8); "a Jesuit Ignatius an apotheosis of falsity, a kind of subtle quintessence and deadly virus of lying" (p. 9); "the apple full formed was ignorance, abasement, and bigotry" (p. 10); "follies and obscenities" (p. 12); "falsehood and perjury, lying and false swearing, were allowable" (p. 13); "perverted principles, unchaste habits, and inordinate love of gain" (p. 13); "handing on to the bloody enterprise" (p. 14); "cunning and cruelty" (p. 15); "cunning, villiany [*sic*], lying and thieving propensities" (p. 16); and throughout.

Jesuits. 37

declared his opinion that many of these men had through various means crept into the fold, in the following terms : " There are at this moment *many Jesuits, concealed, of course, but still acting as Church of England clergymen*, and in the possession of parishes, who are silently but surely working its downfall."

Space will not permit me to give further extracts from this pamphlet, which shows incidentally that the Jesuits were responsible for the burning of Latimer and Ridley, the Franco-Prussian war, " all our difficulties in Ireland," " the insurrection in Italy," and so on ; " Spain groans beneath the yoke of Loyola and his legion ; every Romish country is under their tread, and all Protestants are harassed."[1] Assuredly, if the question were now asked—

Who fills the butchers' shops with large blue flies?

there could be but one answer.

It is hardly necessary to adduce further evidence to show that the Jesuits are in close alliance with the Ritualists—most Protestant writers are aware of it, and the fact that neither the Jesuits themselves nor the Anglicans would allow that it is so, is evidence of its truth. It is indeed capable of proof. The anonymous writer—a woman—of *The Half-way House, or the Sign of the New Jesuitical Hostelrie* (1894),[2] points out that a translation of *The Hidden Life*, which is published by Rivington and advertised in the *English Catholic's Library*, was written by Père Grou, a

---

[1] At the National Protestant Congress at Preston in 1895, Mr. A. H. Guinness, then Secretary of the Protestant Alliance, showed that the Jesuits were also at the bottom of the war in Switzerland, and conspirators against the institutions of France. See also p. 63, footnote.

[2] It is somewhat surprising that Messrs. Simpkin & Marshall are the publishers of this book, which one would expect to find among Mr. Kensit's publications.

Jesuit. This is, therefore, a pretty clear indication and *a proof of the assertion* [1] that the Roman Catholics are Jesuits, and that the latter are introducing through the Ritualists all the forms and doctrines and their especial creed. . . . I do most earnestly implore all English people who love their country and freedom, to arouse themselves to the fact that Ritualism, Romanism, and Jesuitism are one and the same thing.[2]

The author of this book was a Ritualist for ten years, and her testimony is thus supported by Lord Robert Montagu :—

A few years ago a sharp controversy was carried on by a Jesuit writer, who impugned the statement of Mr. Cartwright, Member for Oxfordshire, as to the existence of "Crypto-Jesuits," or Jesuits who pretended to be Protestants. There was, at that very time, a band of those gentlemen in London, who posed as Protestants, who were always sneering at the Church of England, and rarely went to church.[3] They engaged much in political affairs, and especially in foreign policy ; but their chief employment was making acquaintances and friends, in whom they laboured to implant ideas, or a course of thought, which would inevitably lead to Romanism. At intervals of months or years they would successively implant those ideas, but not in the logical order in which they would appear in the course of thought which they were framing. The result was that, in time, one after another of their friends and acquaintances went over to the Church of Rome.[4]

In a speech delivered in Exeter Hall, on May 14, 1886, Lord Robert enlarged on this subject, quoting the instance of a lady who made a confession to her doctor that " she was not only a Roman Catholic, but

[1] Italics mine.
[2] *The Half-way House*, pp. 82, 83.
[3] If these indications are characteristic of the Crypto-Jesuits, the members of that body are undoubtedly extremely numerous.
[4] Lord Robert Montagu's *Reasons for Leaving the Church of Rome*. Kensit. (No date.)

a Jesuit," and that "*while in the Church of England* she had become affiliated to the Jesuits, and that she had taken the Jesuits' oath over the communion-table at the hands of the Protestant rector of the parish, who was himself a Jesuit in secret correspondence with Rome."

This brings us to the consideration of the Jesuit individually rather than collectively. But I must first quote a delightful letter[1] which Dr. Washington Gladden, the pastor of the First Congregational Church in Columbus, Ohio, sent to an Orangeman who—annoyed that Dr. Gladden had defended Catholics against certain slanders—wrote to ask him why he refused to acknowledge to the world that he had become a Jesuit. It will show that, in spite of the weighty testimony adduced, there are still some who refuse to be convinced of the danger in their midst.

> MY DEAR SIR,—How did you find it out? It is marvellous—the enterprise of your fraternity. But you hadn't heard that I am to be the next Pope, had you? Well, you'll hear that pretty soon. It's part of the bargain. But don't tell it till you are dead sure that it's so. There is another little piece of news that you'll be glad to get. Just as soon as I am elected Pope, that massacre is going to begin which Leo ordered, you know, but which the faithful hadn't the backbone to carry out. Perhaps it was the heroism of the Mayor of Toledo that prevented it. But when I get there it's going through, sure pop. We have engaged the public gardens at Washington down by the monument, and we are going to make a pile of corpses of Protestant ministers, in the form of a pyramid, higher than the top of that monument. It will take, according to my figures, 346,927 ministers to make this heap. There are not enough now in this country, but several new theological seminaries will be started at

[1] Reprinted in *Catholic News*, October 26, 1895.

once (by the Jesuits, of course) to furnish the supply. We've got the railroads chartered to haul 'em from all parts of the country. Aren't you a minister yourself? Well, you'll be in it. I'll try to keep a place near the top for you. Apex reserved for former admirers. And when the pile is complete, I'm going to mount to the top of it and sit there and howl! Now you just take this down to the next meeting of the council and read it to 'em. It'll thrill 'em—you'll see. If anybody says he doesn't believe it you know what's the matter with him. He's a Jesuit!

There are a good many Jesuits in *Beatrice, or the Unknown Relatives,* by Catherine Sinclair. I do not know whether this book is still in print, but it must have had considerable success in its day, judging from the publisher's "advertisement" prefixed to another of this lady's works—*London Homes* :—[1]

The reception given to *Beatrice* in America has exceeded that of *Uncle Tom's Cabin* in England. About 100,000 copies were sold in a few weeks. A pamphlet was published by twenty-eight clergy of New York, advising that each member of their congregation should possess a copy. It has been recommended from the pulpit, and favourable notices have appeared in 500 newspapers and magazines, all of which testify to the deep interest of the story, as well as to the very important object it has in view.

This object—and here I quote from the preface to *Beatrice*—

is to portray, for the consideration of young girls now

---

[1] *London Homes* also contains much information about the ways of the Jesuits—here is a specimen : " It is notorious that the most diabolical tricks have been resorted to by Jesuits in the case of dying men. The sick-chamber has been suddenly filled with flames and sulphureous vapours as a warning to the impertinent [*sic*] sinner, whose better judgment and natural sense of duty withstood their perfidious wiles to obtain his fortune. If he still resisted, the evil spirit himself, in the most frightful shape, has appeared to the dying man as if waiting for his soul."

first emerging into society, the enlightened happiness derived from the religion of England, founded on the Bible, contrasted with the misery arising from the superstitions of Italy, founded on the Breviary; and, in exemplifying both from the best authorities, it has been done in a most careful and laborious reference to the standard authors of the English Church and of the Romish persuasion.

The following are a few of the more striking incidents of the story. The Rev. Mr. Talbot, who was engaged to superintend the education of the young heir of Clanmarina, was "apparently the most Protestant of Protestant tutors, recommended by several Protestant families of distinction, and by more than one Protestant clergyman at Oxford. Never was there such a piece of still life in any house as this learned treasure—a perfect dungeon of knowledge, if he had anything in him at all. He seemed neither to see, to hear, to eat, nor to speak, but made his appearance in society a self-contained man." By his "dark still glance," he "evidently ruled his pupil's very thoughts," and "watched him with an eye that seemed never to slumber." Sir Evan M'Alpine disliked Mr. Talbot—"his reserve," he said, "casts a great black shadow on our spirits whenever he appears." The tutor had a way of "stealthily" slipping out daily "at the very earliest peep of morning light," and took this opportunity of visiting Father Eustace, the chaplain at Eaglescairn Castle, who was a Jesuit. Need it be added that Mr. Talbot also belonged to the Society, and that he perverted his pupil? His stealthy step, his "singular quietude of voice," his "dark still glance," his "strange unaccountable smile," the "profound meaning in his very silence,"—all these showed that there was but too much ground for Lady

Edith's[1] suspicions that Mr. Talbot was "one of that mysterious and most formidable brotherhood, for they would enter a Protestant family, promising, like the Paris boarding-schools, to teach 'every accomplishment and any religion that may be preferred.'"

Sir Evan, Allan's uncle, endeavoured to ascertain Mr. Talbot's views regarding Popery, but in vain: "that silent gentleman took no more audible part in the discussion than the tea-urn." But at last a direct appeal from the worthy baronet—who had playfully taunted Mr. Talbot with his silence by remarking, "If speech was given us, as Rousseau said, to conceal our thoughts, no doubt silence does it still better "— elicited a remark from the priest, whereupon

Sir Evan became plunged in deep thought now for several minutes, after which he added, with his penetrating eyes fixed on his very inscrutable guest, who looked, if it were possible to imagine such a thing of such a man, greatly embarrassed, "Your answer might have been given by a descendant of Delphic oracles, but it does not relieve my mind. The avowed object of every Jesuit is to render each layman a mere puppet in the hands of his priest, with no more free-will than an empty suit of clothes, to think, act, eat, drink, or sleep, only at the will of another mortal man—like himself, also, a sinner. Let Allan, therefore, have an enlightened knowledge of all the unbounded evils of Popery, that he may be prepared for that struggle between truth and superstition which is becoming every year more active in England—which will remain alive now, with increasing vigour, conquering or to be conquered, so long as Britain continues an island; and respecting which the present generation seem likely, in all probability, to leave behind them a legacy of bloodshed, anarchy, and death, to those who inherit the penalty of a fatal confidence in those Jesuits, who will betray every trust, except that of

[1] Lady Edith is the Abdiel of the story, and her unflinching Protestantism is beyond all praise.

Jesuits. 43

their Superior, and every authority, except that of their own Church."

"The effect of Sir Evan's frank open-hearted speech to Mr. Talbot was like that of sunshine on vinegar, making him only fifty times sourer than before." The Jesuit soon afterwards retired, "with a profound meaning in his very silence," and next morning took up his residence with Lord Eaglescairn, the Catholic peer to whose family Father Eustace was confessor. Father Eustace "sold indulgences when the Roman Catholics could afford to purchase any, and impoverished the poorest by his commanding extortions. . . . He reaped from the superstition of these credulous villagers a better rent than Lord Eaglescairn did from their industry, as he had terrified them into paying their little all for an imaginary release from a shadowy Purgatory."

Mr. Talbot, though no longer a resident, continued his visits to the Castle, in spite of Lady Edith, who "again and again found him with Allan, eating luncheon and talking Jesuitism with no more reference to her presence than if she had been a picture." Sir Evan had died, and "the discouragement given by Lady Edith produced no more apparent effect than a flake of snow on the summit of Mont Blanc." This naturally annoyed her ladyship, who took refuge in the utterance of dark sayings, such as, "The block from which to cut a Jesuit should be adamant."

Allan had to meet his father and mother in Rome, and Mr. Talbot offered to accompany him. Before they started, it turned out that Mr. Talbot was no other than Allan's uncle, who in his youth "was adopted by a Popish relative, who promised that he should be brought up a Protestant, but who placed him to be educated in the Jesuits' College at St. Omer." The revelation of this relationship strengthened the confidence which existed between him and Allan, and the latter said, "His character is so strictly upright that he means to set the leaning tower at Pisa straight as we pass it;" to which Lady Edith—who must have been a student of *Proverbial Philosophy*—rejoined, "The adder may change his skin, but the poison remains."

Allan went to Rome, became a Catholic, and returned, broken in health, in charge of his uncle, Mr. Ambrose (formerly Talbot). He was on the eve of signing a deed devoting all his property to the Jesuits, but a providential fall from his horse and subsequent illness prevented this calamity. He was taken to Lady Edith's, and that good lady was successful in preventing Father Eustace's access to the sick-room. There was a spirited scene between the two, which terminated as follows:—

"You are refusing the privileges of the Church to one of her most devoted proselytes, and braving all the frightful consequences of doing so," said Father Eustace, in a tone of suppressed fury. "It would be Sir Allan's first wish, if he dies, to secure his own salvation by dying in the habit of our Order."

"And while doing so," said Lady Edith, drily, yet almost smiling at the priest's self-satisfied audacity, "to leave your Order all his property, present or to come. Really, sir, I most heartily wish, for the sake of peace at Clanmarina, that the Pope would abdicate in your favour. There would be at Rome a wider scope afforded to your genius for priestly domination."

"Infernal heretic!" muttered Father Eustace, malignantly. "For your own sake remember that to affront a priest is one of those sins for which there is in our Church no absolution. We term it a reserved case."

Jesuits.

Sir Allan's illness brings us into contact with Mrs. Lorraine, a "Jesuitess."[1] She made her appearance earlier in the story in the guise of a Protestant governess, but the watchful Lady Edith had her eye upon her. "These Jesuits," she said, "always wish to ensnare the young, and I would rather see one of Shrapnel's shells explode in this house than receive a Jesuit into it." Finding that Mrs. Lorraine had been distributing books to the children, she asked to see them. " A display of literature took place such as Lady Edith in her wildest dreams could not have apprehended. Each scholar had received a tract to exchange weekly, containing the life of some half-crazed monk or nun, who had forsaken every duty of life. . . . These tracts were all enclosed in the covers which had been lent for the Protestant stories which had hitherto been provided by Mr. Clinton to the children, and had exactly the same external aspect as the *Parent's Assistant*, or *Tales of a Grandfather*"—from which we gather that the tracts of that period must have been considerably more bulky than those of the present day. They must also, it is to be feared, have been inaccurate in historical detail, for one, *The Life of St. Dominick*, had " a frontispiece representing the Saint carrying his head under his arm." Lady Edith, after a speech in which she said, "I need not reproach you for this breach of trust, having discovered that you belong to an Order which keeps no faith with those who differ from themselves," added, "we part now and for ever."

Subsequent events, however, showed that on this

---

[1] "Mrs. Lorraine is a Jesuit, or what is ten times worse, a Jesuitess," said a shrewd old Scotchman, whose eagle eye detected the attempted deception.

occasion Lady Edith was not a true prophet. For a time Mrs. Lorraine set up an "opposition school upon the most attractive plan, with a tea-party on Saturday to all the pupils," as well as an "extremely fascinating little bazaar," where she sold statues, pictures, and tracts—a sort of Catholic Truth Society depôt. She also influenced the clergyman, Mr. Clinton, although the traditional wisdom of her Order was hardly justified by her presenting that gentleman with the *Glories of Mary*. She then reappeared as the Abbess of St. Ignatia, "with her hands buried under the folds of her long serge dress, and distinguished from the nuns only by a heavy gold cross"—at Clanmarina she wore a "shabby gown and unspeakable bonnet"—and "Beatrice, with a start of astonishment, recognized in the Abbess the everywhere-present Mrs. Lorraine." The convent over which this lady presided was one of the good old sort, containing a nun so carefully imprisoned that a casual visitor could hear her say: "Do I once more hear the voice of strangers? Long years have passed away and still I am here. Oh, let me be released;" while another nun described to another visitor how she had been pulled along the floor by the hair and kicked several times by the Abbess, after which she was kept for two days without food, and tied to the wall by her hair for a week; besides being occasionally shut up for twenty days with her face to a white-washed wall.

Mrs. Lorraine's next appearance, and final encounter with Lady Edith, was as follows. Dr. Campbell had sent a nurse from Inverness to attend to Sir Allan: "she complained of a severe toothache, and sat rolled up in an enormous shawl, with her cap drawn over her face." Sir Allan, who had been progressing favourably, suddenly relapsed. That night, Beatrice, who was sitting up with Lady Edith, heard a low murmuring noise, which seemed to proceed from the sick-chamber.

Noiselessly and cautiously Beatrice advanced along the passage. She followed the sound, pushed the door imperceptibly open, and discovered the room brilliantly illuminated with six large wax candles surrounding a stucco image of the Virgin Mary. Sir Allan was supported on his knees in bed by Mrs. Lorraine, and Father Eustace stood holding up an ebony cross for him to kiss. . . . Beside the bed lay Mrs. Lorraine's bead-remembrancer. . . . While she stood there panic-struck, Sir Allan asked, in a fainting voice, "Does the doctor order me no wine to-day? I feel sinking so rapidly."

"No," replied Mrs. Lorraine. "His instructions are that you keep the season of fasting as a faithful son of our Church."

The patient looked both surprised and disappointed, but made no reply; and Beatrice, who knew how earnestly the doctor had enjoined wine, or even brandy, listened in silent horror to this lie so coolly told for the good of the Popish Church.

She flew off to Lady Edith, who "in an instant comprehended rather than guessed that the sick-nurse from Inverness had accepted a bribe from Mrs. Lorraine to let her own place be assumed by herself, that indefatigable worker in the Jesuit school." The two went to the sick-room, and, finding that the two Jesuits were in the dressing-room, locked them in, and they were let out by a back door. "Lady Edith had found in a place of concealment the wine, brandy, and food, which Sir Allan was supposed to have taken during the previous day, when he was, in fact, superstitiously keeping the strictest fast of Friday, as instigated by Mrs. Lorraine." The judicious administration of these saved his life. *Beatrice* ends with a picture of Mrs. Lorraine in a new capacity :—

"I hear that a retreat is about to be opened immediately in Charlotte Square, by Mrs. Lorraine," said Lady Anne. "Not an absolute nunnery, but in a half-and-half state, where a full-dress rehearsal is allowed to young candidates for the veil, who retire there to ascertain how they like to play at monks [?] and nuns. The whole affair is to be made as agreeable to them as novelty, romance, and flattery can render such a life, till they are enticed onwards to take the irrevocable vows, and after that the curtain drops for ever."

I fear the curtain must also drop over Clanmarina, so far as its Jesuits are concerned, although I shall have something to say later of its laity. I am sorry to have made so little of Father Eustace, whose career is full of striking events, and whose personal habits were sufficiently remarkable to demand notice.[1] But I must pass on to a more recent narrative, *John Drummond Fraser*, "a story of Jesuit Intrigue in the Church of England," by Philalethes.[2]

---

[1] On one occasion he stood "immovable, like an Egyptian mummy"; on another, he "stood in the position of a perpendicular corpse, his eyes closed, his mouth pursed in, his hands folded together, his feet ranged side by side, and his whole figure crouching with assumed humility." Perpendicular crouching must be difficult. He was also in the habit of "emptying [his people's] purses with a face of brass, and dividing their families with a heart of steel." Once he appeared "attired in the full costume of his order, a black robe in the form of a toga, with a cross worked in gold on the right breast." On this occasion he "muttered between his teeth": it is painful to add that his mutterings had reference to Lady Edith, of whom he observed, "The old heretic! I could willingly thrust her alive into that fire and stamp upon her!" Having spoken "in a tone of most imperious authority, and holding up his finger in a menacing attitude," he "advanced with his usual noiseless velvet step, while his glittering eyes looked cold as steel at Lady Edith." Every right-minded person will rejoice to know that in that noble woman he met his match. "Lady Edith listened in dignified attention, but with a penetrating look that made Father Eustace cast down his eyes and become as silent as if he had been a stone statue of himself, and as if his mind had been marble."

[2] Cassell & Co., 1893.

John Drummond Fraser was a kind of amateur city missionary, and in the course of his work became acquainted with a begging-letter writer, named Lacelles [*sic*]. Lacelles ran away with somebody else's wife, and "joined the Romish Church while at Rome with her." He gave Fraser the following account of his career:—

"After she died I soon ran through all the money I had in bad company. I was then persuaded by the Jesuits to join them, and was admitted into their Society. My knowledge of the Church of England would be useful to them. They did not treat me well, and when in England with information for Father Bellarmini, I did not return, but let my beard grow, and hid myself, and, with forged testimonials, taught in private schools for some years. That was found out, and I fled to London, shaving my face and getting men to disguise me. I don't consider I am a Romanist now. Let me tell you about Father Bellarmini. He is a wonderful man, but don't get into his bad books. Romanist or English Churchman he can bite, if he does not get his way. His rule is iron, and the management and planning that goes on down there in Westernshire, would open your eyes to see how the Jesuits are undermining the liberty of England. I have a list of converts to Rome who have gone over privately, and no one knows but what they are still English Church people. Father Bellarmini manages all that and gives dispensations; I would sell that list if I could get a good sum for it."

Fraser, who was naturally impressed by this interesting information, then wrote to an excellent Protestant minister, who replied in a very long letter containing further details regarding the work of the Society:—

There in England they flourish, and are rapidly winding their net around the liberties of the nation. They are on the staffs of our newspapers, they serve as footmen in the mansions of noblemen, they adopt the garb of the

British workman, they hold curacies, if not livings, in the Church of England, and at our Universities they have managed to introduce a faction which defiantly avows its determination to lead the National Church back to the Papacy. . . . England lets them work, and flatters their leading prelates, even calling them saintly. . . .

Fraser came across the curate of Danbicombe, Charles Mildmay, in whom he "became aware of a want of straightforwardness he could not understand or fathom." Alas!—supported by "a Ritualistic banker," by "a man known as the 'antiquarian' of the district," and by an "easygoing" rector,—Mildmay, "in anything but a straightforward manner, began the unhappily too well-known succession of changes in the services of our parish churches." Fraser went to a dinner-party, at which he delivered the most marvellous and most lengthy of speeches ever made on such an occasion, but all in vain. Even Lady Raynald—whose husband, Sir George, was "an outspoken blunt Protestant"—went to confession, and filled her dressing-room with "crucifixes, pictures of saints, and books of prayers and penances." "Sir George gave way to a fit of passion," wrote to Fraser, went to Mildmay (whom he forbade to enter his house or grounds), "and swore with an oath (the first he had uttered for years), that every time he found his wife had been to the confessional, he would horsewhip Mildmay with all his strength. . . . He wrote to the Bishop, but matters were made worse."

Meanwhile, Fraser, at greater length than ever, was converting Miss Mildmay from scepticism, while Lacelles was in fear for his life. A man had taken a small shop near him, and, although he had no need whatever for help, employed an assistant. "This

Jesuits.   51

assistant, I find," says Lacelles to Fraser, "is just some one to watch me;" and his letter had to be sent by messenger, as " the man at the shop has succeeded in getting the post-office, and no letters must be allowed to pass through his hands." Lacelles possessed papers of great importance to the Jesuits, "the publication of which would be a terrible blow to some of those in power."

"They know that I have them, but they feel sure that I can tell where they are. [This seems somewhat confused.] If they can find me, I must either disclose what I know, or die, struck down from behind. My disappearance just at the time when those papers were wanted was a trouble to them, especially to Bellarmini. His fine face would put on anything but his usual saintly expression were I to whisper in his ear that I had those papers, and was going to send them to the rightful owners in Italy. . . . His knowledge that I can find them, and use them to his destruction, preserves my life."

Under these circumstances, Lacelles suggested that he should come to see Fraser. Fraser said, "Let us pray over this matter;" and Sir George, who, through Fraser's "earnest entreaties, kept his hands off Mildmay," said, "Let Lacelles come." So he came, having, by means of "a series of short journeys round," eluded both the man of the small shop and his unnecessary assistant. Fraser at once prepared to enter into a conversation, but Lacelles, knowing what this meant, wisely replied, "You are my host, but you will not mind my saying that, after three weeks of dodging, you must let me go to bed." But before he went he said a word or two about Bellarmini.

"I am bitter, vindictive, perhaps. I would like to beat Bellarmini to a jelly. Did he not take away my love from me, and drive her about in his carriage? [And this in Rome!] Did he not, by the confessional, make her hate me and learn to love him? One of the reasons I allowed myself to be persuaded into joining the society of St. Vincent de Paul, and becoming a *Paolotto*, was that I might learn how to follow him, and have my revenge."

Refreshed by his night's rest, Lacelles was able in the morning to demonstrate to Fraser and Sir George that, "having friends as well as foes amongst the Order of St. Vincent de Paul," he "knew a good deal more, perhaps, than you would give him credit for." He explained that Lady Raynald's large fortune would go to the Jesuits "if she could be persuaded to join the Romish Church"; and pointed out that "the snares of semi-Popery" were being laid to secure her. Sir George this time commendably abstained from swearing, but said, "Can this possibly be a fact?" to which Lacelles replied, "To Englishmen it seems impossible that it can be true; but it is only because they won't read." Sir George refused to believe that Mildmay was "doing Rome's work in the Church of England"; to which Lacelles returned, "The Church of England is honey-combed with Jesuits." Mildmay, he explained, "was won over to Rome at a well-known theological College, persuaded to remain in the Church of England, and was sent here to spread Romish doctrine in this district; but specially to lay his nets for the gold which they must have, and which Lady Raynald is known to possess in such abundance." Bellarmini was Mildmay's father confessor, and Mildmay went once a month to him to receive instructions, at the same time repeating Lady Raynald's confession.

The current of the story is here interrupted by forty pages of theological discussion between Mildmay and Fraser, and then we come to Father Bellarmini—

Jesuits. 53

"an assumed name, of course; his real name might have been Smith, Jones, or Robinson, for undoubtedly he was English by birth, though completely Italianized in name and bearing." With him were Father Clemini, from Rome, and Father Torado. Bellarmini, who was strikingly handsome,—

had an open hand as to the way he formed his plans for spreading Romanism in England, only he was to leave no stone unturned to assist in subjugating once more the British Crown to the See of Rome. . . . His face lighted up in anticipation of approaching victory; he was not in company that he need fear to throw off all reserve, and he spoke with almost impassioned tones of the news he was able to impart, that the Cardinal Archbishop had that day been accorded precedence over the Archbishop of Canterbury.

"Our chief difficulty," Bellarmini explained, "is in the Bible-reading habits of the middle and lower classes;" and an interesting conversation ensued, which was interrupted by the announcement that "Brother Gregory had arrived, and craved an audience of the Holy Father."

"The Holy Father" was not the Pope, but Bellarmini: and Brother Gregory, as my readers will have guessed, was Charles Mildmay. While he was in the train, he had dressed himself in a cassock and a cloak, and had also put on "another kind of soft felt hat, more slouchy, wider brimmed, and more Romish than the other." In this guise he walked to the Jesuit mansion, resisting a powerful temptation to fling himself under a luggage train; "might he not say a short prayer and go to Purgatory at once?" He arrived at the door, "and a voice said some words in Latin, to which he replied *Pax vobiscum*, and the gate was unlocked."

Brother Gregory stayed there several days, but

Bellarmini was unable to minister satisfactorily to his diseased mind. So he went again to Fraser. "It was just at this juncture that God stepped in and did for him what he could not, dared not, attempt in his present condition." He was thrown from a dog-cart, carried back to Orchard Lodge, where Fraser read to him from the Bible and Miss Havergal's hymns. In spite of this he recovered, and when "two apparently very advanced Ritualistic priests" came to see him—they were really Bellarmini and Clemini—Fraser protected him from their machinations. Bellarmini said he had been summoned by letter; but that letter was written by Lacelles, whose conduct can only be excused by his having belonged to two Religious Orders and also been educated at Stonyhurst. There was a terrible scene. Lacelles produced the documents, and said, "Your game is up, and you know it," and "in silence the two Jesuits left Orchard Lodge." Mildmay got well; "he confessed [not, however, this time to 'the Holy Father,' but] to Sir George and Lady Raynald that all his work had been at the suggestion and under the supervision of Father Bellarmini, and that he was but one among many others who were carrying on similar propaganda in other parishes throughout the country." Fraser married the no longer sceptical Miss Mildmay, and on bidding his brother-in-law good-bye, put a paper into his hand containing an assortment of texts; and so the story ends.

It will hardly be believed that this preposterous work, the impossible literary style of which will have been made manifest by my quotations, was reviewed at length by the *Daily Chronicle*, which considered that the author had entirely proved his case!

Jesuits.

I now proceed to give a brief analysis of *Nightshade*: a novel by no less a person than Mr. William Johnston, M.P. for Ballykilbeg, which was published first in 1857 and re-issued in 1895. The Jesuit—who personated a dead gentleman named Aubrey de Vere—comes on the scene at the very beginning of the book: a "pale-faced raven-haired figure," who makes himself unpleasant to the two twin nieces of Aubrey de Vere, who fall into his clutches. When their trusty old retainer interested himself in their future, the Jesuit "answered in but one word and that one word was—'Begone!'" Anna fell into a waterfall—I think the Jesuit was responsible for this—and was rescued by Charles Annandale; and De Vere, instead of seeing that the poor girl was properly attended to, "stood silently by her bedside, as if he were mentally anatomizing a corpse." Mr. M'Intosh, an excellent but prosy minister and uncle by marriage to Anna and her sister, told Charles all about the Oxford movement and its leaders, who, said the worthy man, "are Jesuits—Jesuits in disguise ; men who, to subserve the interest of the Church of Rome, would lie, forge, commit perjury, anything, in short, that their order required them to do"; "I could tell you," he added, "things about that order that would make you doubt whether Jesuits are men or demons."

Then we suddenly find ourselves in Ireland, where Pat Grimes and Frank Higgins arrange with Father O'Toole to murder a man who has been "named at the althar," after which, the sum necessary for obtaining absolution having been duly handed over, Pat "was absolved from the guilt of the thing that he intended to do, by the reverend Father O'Toole."

How she got there we are not told, but we next find Emily "weeping in her little bed in a convent in

Paris," where she was "prisoned and fed." De Vere managed to get Anna's letter to her suppressed; and Emily was apparently hypnotized into becoming a nun, under the singular misapprehension that she was going home: "Every step in the ceremony she thought of, not as part of the thing they called a Benediction, but as a step nearer home." But when it was all over, and she told Sister Mary she was leaving, Sister Mary "laughed 'Ha! ha! ha!' gaily," until Sister Rosa remarked with asperity, but not, it would seem, without some justification, "Sister Mary, be done! you are laughing like an idiot!" Then the Mother Abbess hit Emily twice over the head with her rosary and crucifix, and stuck her scissors[1] into her cheek. Thus early did Emily discover that conventual life is not all beer and skittles.

Then Mr. M'Intosh brought an action against the false Aubrey de Vere for abducting Emily and appropriating the family property, and the way in which the Jesuit was shown up by Mr. Martin, the counsel for the plaintiff, was a caution. A secret will turned up, and "the late confident and audacious impostor sat biting his under lip in vain and impotent rage," while his counsel "saw it was all up now, and closed the case hurriedly"; verdict for the plaintiff. Lord Frederick snapped his fingers and said, "That's for those infernal Jesuits!" Charles Annandale only remarked, "Thank God that England's daughters not yet shall be the slaves of Rome!"

As he said this, some one passed behind them, touching Annandale's coat; and as he passed a hissing whisper came

[1] The Abbess wore these "all fastened together and hung by a black silk ribbon; they were easily loosened when she wanted to say an 'Ave,'" or apparently when needed for disciplinary purposes.

forth from his lips. Like a serpent he hissed, though he only said one word, and that one word was "Wait!"—

a word which does not seem to lend itself readily to hissing.

Then a Jesuit was sent to Anna with a bogus letter from Emily, endorsed by the *soi-disant* De Vere, "Emily I fear is dying." So she went off to Paris with the Jesuit, "and there came over his face a strangely compounded smile, one half sardonic and sneering, and the other half a breaking-out consciousness of having before him a good reward." It must take a good deal of practice to work that kind of smile. Meanwhile Emily had a visit from a mad Sister Anna, who indulged her with what she could remember of *Maria Monk*, in the middle of which the Abbess appeared and said, "Stop her mouth, will you?" and they did.

After a while a door opened, away below, and there was a struggling sound of some one being forced in; and then there came a shriek, weird and unearthly, and a wild sounding wail, all along those galleries and into every cell, and with weird, unearthly, wild-sounding wail:—
"No! no! no! no! no!"

Charles Annandale and John Connell made their way to Paris, and found the convent, which belonged "to a sister order that did the work of the Jesuits in the female educational line." "The Abbess received them with politeness; she did not forget her rosary, her crucifix, and her scissors," although she did not then employ them as instruments of percussion. But she wouldn't let them see Emily; so they said three times, "This is infernal work!" and went straight off to the British Ambassador. Alas! his Excellency had been nobbled by the false De Vere, so they took nothing by that move, and went back to England. Then Annandale sounded the praises of the Orange Society as "the only honest political creed, because it is never changed, being based upon true Protestantism," and moreover having the honour of being hated by the Jesuits; and Father O'Toole burnt a lot of Bibles, "an acceptable offering made at the shrine of the gods that were worshipped by [him]."

After this we go to Scotland, where they know all about the Jesuits. Sandie Campbell said, "They scheme an' plot an' pretend to be what they are no at a'; an' they be sairvants o' the pope an' the deevil." He mentioned this to a stranger, who spoke of him in consequence as "an ill-mannered fellow"; need I say that this was the false De Vere?

Meanwhile poor Anna was put into "a dark and cold place," with "sharp-pointed stones jutting out," and a "dull sound of flowing water" somewhere close by. "The Abbess and the pale-faced Jesuit" came to look at her.

"Will you agree now to my proposal?" said the latter.[1]
"To become a nun?"
"Yes."
"Never!"
"Ha! not tamed yet?"
"I will never become a nun; I told you so before."
"We shall see."

. . . .

"And so you refuse to become a nun?"
"I do."
"Think again."
"I have told you I never will be a nun."
"To join Emily?"

[1] The curious will not fail to observe the resemblance between Mr. Johnston's dialogues and those of the "penny dreadful."

"Oh! cease!"
"Do you care for Emily?"
"This is cruel."
"She longs to see you."
"Ha! thanks; you told me this all before. You deceived me; it was false then; it is false now. You may do what you please; I will never be a nun."
"You shall!"
"Never!"
"I have said."

Then the Abbess and the Jesuit went upstairs.

One would like to say something about "Mr. Tractate," who "was accustomed to perform something which he looked upon as an act of worship, at certain stated periods during the day, before a *large* crucifix," and who kept "the vigil of St. Solomon." One of his pupils was so delighted to find his tailor's bill headed "Eve of St. Judas," that he paid it at once.

One student got such a veneration for saints, that he had discovered that every day in the year was dedicated to some saint or other. He was preparing a pamphlet accordingly, which was to prove to the people of England that they should keep holy the saints' days, and not work upon them; and then he went on to give a catalogue of the three hundred and sixty-five saints who had each his separate day, on which it was a highly reprehensible thing to do any work of any sort whatever. Another young gentleman adopted Mr. Tractate's view on the subject of monasteries, and declared that it was the strongest proof of the sinful nature of man that Adam and Eve, when they had eaten the forbidden fruit, did not go into a monastery at once.

Mr. Tractate was, of course, a Jesuit in the disguise of an Anglican clergyman.

Then we get an insight into convent conversation.

"What a pity she won't die!" said Sister Mary Joseph, just finishing an *Ave Maria*.

"Those English girls are very hard to kill. If she had been a French girl she would have died mad long ago," replied Sister Mary Teresa.

But the confessor knew better than to let Emily—for it was she—die.

"We must try and keep her alive if we can."
"Why, reverend father?".
"She is not yet of age according to the English law."
"What matter? cannot she live till then, whether she die or not?"
"It would not avail to try that plan twice."
"It has been often done," urged the Abbess.
"That I know; but these English are dreadfully suspicious."
"What shall we do, then?" asked the Abbess anxiously.

They agreed to send her to a convent in England, and, before she went, the Abbess tried to induce Emily to have "the confessor," "knowing that she would hear all, notwithstanding the pretended secrecy of the confessional." But Emily was too sharp for her, and said:—

"No."
"Will you confess to-morrow?"
"No; I am too weak yet."
"You are quite strong now."
"I don't want the confessor."
"I must put a penance on you then for neglect of duty."

"But the Abbess did not mind the penance:" most of us are similarly indifferent to troubles that do not affect ourselves, but I fancy "mind" here means "remember"—Mr. Johnston's nationality sometimes betrays itself.

They smuggled Emily over to England, and she put her head out of the carriage window and screamed;

but one of the Jesuits said she was an escaped lunatic, and the other pressed his hand over her mouth, so poor Emily was sold again.

Then the Italians drove the Jesuits out of Rome, and there was a general smash-up, in the course of which Annandale got into the buildings of the Inquisition, where he found lots of human bones and "a long silky tress of golden hair." The false De Vere—whose real name was Ricci—got finished off at last, in spite of his "crossing himself to St. Ignatius and our Lady." Annandale and several other persons broke into the convent where he was. Here they found more human bones, and Anna, whose "long thin fingers were cold—cold—cold." The Jesuit "struck at Annandale's stooping form," but a Roman was too quick for him.

"'Die, villain!' he exclaimed, as over the two prostrate forms [of Anna and Annandale] the Jesuit fell; and the Jesuit, Ricci, died"—apparently out of sheer anxiety to oblige the Roman, for he doesn't seem to have been injured in any way.

Charles Annandale and "fifty stalwart men" broke into the convent where Emily was confined, and found her "creeping along the wall, a thin pale figure, clad in the dismal dress of the nun-slaves of Rome." "The Abbess stood at the gate and crosssd herself, mingling maledictions and *Ave Marias*," but they took Emily away, and the bells rang "Dingle, dangle, dong; dingle, dangle, dong," while the "brave honest Englishmen again and again repeated, 'Hurrah! Hurrah! Hurrah!'" But Emily died all the same, while Anna married Annandale, and no doubt lived happy ever after.

Before leaving the Jesuits, I must refer to Charles

Kingsley's brilliant and unfair story, *Westward Ho!* which I am inclined to think, from its well-deserved popularity (speaking from a literary standpoint) and large circulation, has done much mischief among the young—and not only among the young—for several generations. I have myself, when deprecating certain attacks upon the Society, been met by quotations from this book, as though Kingsley's reputation for accuracy had never been called in question. A few years ago a well-known South London clergyman, preaching in a City pulpit, referred to the Jesuits in the West Indies as being in the habit of baptizing the children of the natives and then killing them. Knowing him slightly, I wrote to ask his authority for so alarming a statement. I at once received a courteous reply, in which the writer expressed regret for having said anything to which exception could be taken, and cited as his authority—*Westward Ho!* The passage, of which my correspondent had an imperfect memory, was no doubt the following :—

One, catching the pretty babe out of my arms, calls for water and a priest (for they had their shavelings with them), and no sooner was it christened than, catching the babe by the heels, he dashed out its brains against the ground ; and so did they to several more innocents that night, after they had christened them ; saying it was best for them to go to heaven while they were still sure thereof.[1]

In this passage, it is true, the Jesuits are not specified, but the following is sufficiently definite :—

He was an Indian [who] had been stolen as a boy by some Spaniards, who had gone down (as was the fashion of

---

[1] Ch. vii.

the Jesuits even as late as 1790) for the pious purpose of converting the savages by the simple process of catching, baptizing, and making servants of those whom they could carry off, and murdering those who resisted their gentle method of salvation.[1]

And again :—

. . . Those much-boasted Jesuit missions in which (as many of them as existed anywhere but on paper) military tyranny was superadded to monastic, and the Gospel preached with fire and sword, almost as shamelessly as by the first Conquistadores.[2]

Fathers Campion and Parsons are described as "blustering bullies," "a couple of rogues," "gentlemen in no sense in which the word is applied in this book"; the teaching of the Jesuits[3] was "base and vulgar,"[4] and its result on Eustace Leigh (whom "his father had sent to be made a liar of at Rheims") is thus described :—

Eustace is a man no longer; he is become a thing, a tool, a Jesuit; which goes only where it is sent, and does good or evil indifferently as it is bid: which, by an act of moral suicide, has lost its soul in the hope of saving it; without a will, a conscience, a responsibility (as it fancies) to God or man, but only to "The Society."[5]

Father Parsons hears a dying man's confession, which he is unable to understand; whereupon Eustace (who was not a priest), having "returned with the Holy Wafer [one wonders where he got it!], and the

---

[1] Ch. xxi.   [2] Ch. xxv.

[3] A curious illustration of Kingsley's anti-Jesuit prejudice is found in the *Life and Letters of Sir C. J. F. Bunbury*, vol. iii., p. 22 (1895): "Kingsley thinks that the ruin of France under this last Empire was brought about by the priests, and especially the Jesuits, working on the Emperor, through the Empress, over whom they had gained absolute power. He has no doubt that the Emperor was urged on to the German War by the Jesuits."

[4] Ch. iv.   [5] Ch. xxii.

oil for Extreme Unction," "knelt down on the other side of the sufferer, and interpreted his thieves' dialect into Latin."[!]¹ According to this sometime Professor of History, the Penal Laws were never intended to be effective; the "English Martyrs," as Catholics love to call them, owed their fate to their indiscretions, and dwelt in hiding-places because they liked it.²

The penal laws never troubled any one who did not make conspiracy and rebellion an integral doctrine of his religious creed; and they seldom troubled even them, unless, fired with the glory of martyrdom, they bullied the long-suffering of Elizabeth and her council into giving them their deserts, and, like poor Father Southwell in after years, insisted on being hanged, whether Burleigh liked or not. . . . [At the] old house at Morwinstow . . . Jesuits and seminary priests skulked in and out all the year round, unquestioned though unblest; and found a sort of piquant pleasure, like naughty boys who have crept into the store-closet, in living in mysterious little dens in a lonely turret, going up through a trap-door to celebrate Mass in a secret chamber in the roof, where they were allowed by the powers that were to play as much as they chose at persecuted saints, and preach about hiding in dens and caves of the earth.

I am sorry to include a name so honourable in many ways as that of Charles Kingsley among the writers of Protestant fiction; but the extracts I have given—and they might easily be multiplied—more than establish his claim to a place among them.

[1] Ch. xiv.
[2] "We should never have had the law of 1571, against Bulls, and Agnus Deis, and blessed grains, if the Pope's Bull of 1549 had not made them matter of treason:" "What brought Cuthbert Mayne to the gallows, and turned Mr. Trudgeon out of his house and home, but treasonable talk;" "after the law of 1571 was made, it was never put in force till Mayne and Trudgeon made fools of themselves, and that was full six years" (ch. iv.).

III. PRIESTS.

"OF priests we can offer a charming variety," says Mr. Alfred Perceval Graves—himself a Protestant—in his popular song, "Father O'Flynn." The priests of Protestant fiction, however, offer very little variety, and that by no means "charming." Agreeing in their leading characteristics, they differ materially from the priest of the average novel, who is either a jovial, rollicking, good-natured, and not too intelligent Irishman, such as we find in the stories of Charles Lever; or an intellectual, refined being, who cannot look you in the face, and who habitually glides. We have them both in Henry Kingsley's *Ravenshoe*—"a jolly-looking, round-faced, Irish priest, by name Tiernay," who smokes cigars, sings, "in an absent manner, in a sweet, low voice,

'For the girl of my heart that I'll never see more,'"

tells stories "about the five Miss Moriartys" and St. Bridget and the oyster, says "he ain't," and talks of "edication" and "the hooly Church": and Father Mackworth, "of presentable exterior and polite manners," who comes from Rome, and who "in a very few days had gauged every intellect in the house." Father Mackworth "talked about the Immaculate Conception through his nose"; spoke Latin to a brother priest at dinner in mixed company; glided about; opened doors at unexpected times; could not "help lying"; plotted disgracefully; yet refused a bribe of £10,000, although, in some mysterious manner, a "cardinal's chair" would have followed.[1]

Not altogether satisfactory either of them, though the author clearly means us to like Father Tiernay. Father Mackworth had all the characteristics of the stage, or Protestant, Jesuit—and indeed belonged to the Society, although this fact is only incidentally mentioned—among them that of "gliding," a habit cultivated by every Jesuit in fiction worth mention, although, so far as I know them, curiously absent from the living examples. I remember that when making a retreat at Manresa, some three or four years after I had become a Catholic, there seemed a distinct want of fitness in the creaky boots worn by Father Anderdon, the approach of which I could hear when they were quite a long way off.

Among the regular[2] clergy, the Benedictines claim the foremost place, on account of the immuring of nuns, a custom which, it would seem, they were the first to introduce and to embody in their Rule. It is to be regretted that none of those who so glibly repeat this statement, and quote Sir Walter Scott in support of their case, have ever cited the passage in the Rule of St. Benedict which provides for this ceremony. Until this has been done, common-sense folk may be excused for accepting Father Thurston's pamphlet on *The Immuring of Nuns*[3] as

---

[1] "I have refused a cardinal's chair this night." . . . "A cardinal's chair thrown to the dogs" (ch. xxv.).

[2] This familiar term is not always intelligible even to the educated Protestant. Mr. Montagu Fowler, in his book on *Some Notable Archbishops of Canterbury*, states that St. Augustine was accompanied on his mission to this country "by forty monks, secular and regular."

[3] Catholic Truth Society, price 1d

effectively disposing of this Protestant myth. In later times the immuring performance was taken up by the Dominicans, as appears from the testimony of Mr. Rider Haggard and numerous other writers of equal authority. Perhaps, however, the Benedictines still retain an interest in the business, for the "tall priest" who was dressed "in the white robe and hood of the Dominicans that left nothing visible except his eyes"—Mr. Haggard is nothing if not accurate—was assisted at the function by a "black-robed, keen-eyed priest," who used bad language and struck the about-to-be-immured nun with a crucifix.[1] The Dominicans, indeed, come next to the Jesuits in Protestant disfavour, on account of their association with the Inquisition. Subsequently walling-up became so general that even Lady Abbesses could decree its execution[2]; and it passed, as we know, into the great body of tradition which forms the basis of Protestant belief.

Dominicans and Franciscans divide the honours in a tale which has had a wide circulation, *The Six Sisters of the Valleys*, by the Rev. William Bramley-Moore, M.A. This was published in 1864, and has passed through numerous editions.[3] The author, whose acquaintance I was privileged to enjoy, was, at the time he wrote this, incumbent of a Buckinghamshire parish; he subsequently abandoned his cure and

---

[1] *Montezuma's Daughter*, by H. Rider Haggard, chaps. ix., x. See *The Myth of the Walled-up Nun*, by Father Thurston; Catholic Truth Society, price 1d.

[2] See *Falconbridge*—a work to be dealt with later—p. 56.

[3] The whole of the three-volume edition and a large edition of the cheap issue were sold within little more than a year; it was translated into French, Italian, and German, and placed on the catalogue of the Pure Literature Society. See Preface to third edition (1865).

adopted the views of Professor Huxley, after which he joined the "Catholic Apostolic," or Irvingite, community. The plot of the story is simple: six Waldensian sisters married six Waldensian brothers; all were persecuted in various ways by the Papists; some died, but others—I think, for I have never finished the book—survived. My concern is, however, not with these excellent folk, but with the priests who figure in the volume.

In the first chapter we come face to face with the Pope, Innocent X. Having entered the Sala Regia, to which he was conducted by "several acolytes," he ascended the throne, and "said, in a peculiar cadence, *Dominus vobiscum*, and stretching out two fingers of his right hand, made a motion, at which the beholders fell on their knees and crossed themselves." The Pope, having ordered the persecution of the Waldenses, had an uneasy time of it. He went by himself into the Sistine Chapel, "cast himself on his face before the high altar, . . . anon he wandered among the stalls of the choir, and coming back within the rails, knelt on the steps of the altar; but he found no rest." He then "fell down upon the steps, while the broken words fell from him, 'Have mercy on me! Jansenius —did I condemn him? In how many points—five— five? Why will the Jesuits assail me? Avaunt, Olympia, my brother's widow—how many bishopricks hast thou given away? *Kyrie eleison. Maria, Regina Angelorum.*'" A few days after this he died, and "our scene is changed" to the farm of the six brothers and six sisters.

The character with whom I propose mainly to concern myself is the Franciscan Malvicino, "Abbot of Pignerol, Confessor to the Marchioness of Pianesse."

"He was short in stature and somewhat corpulent, while his eyes, dim with sensuality, betrayed rather the revels of the refectory than the vigils of the oratory." Malvicino was chiefly distinguished by the originality and variety of his oaths and his indiscreet zeal for the conversion of heretics. "Leave her to me," he said, "and by Pope Benedict IX., who sold St. Peter's chair, I'll soon make a disciple of her, and add another member to the Holy Catholic and Apostolic Church." But Marie declined to be converted, although the Franciscan did his best. "If you will not let me do it by persuasion," he said at last, "I shall excommunicate you, and hand you over to the soldiers of the Cross." He then called upon Father Placido Corso to "lend [his] spiritual aid to drag this daughter into the kingdom," but Father Placido said:—

"Argue with her out of the Bible; you know enough of it, don't you, to vindicate our doctrines?"
"I don't think I do; I only know some of those parts I chant by heart; and if it comes to bandying texts of Scripture, by Pope Celestine III., who kicked the Emperor Henry VI.'s crown off his head, I shall come off the worst. But go and look after your belongings, and leave me with my erring daughter."

Malvicino went up to Marie, and holding the crucifix against her lips, said: "So you refuse to belong to the Holy Roman Church, and talk about your cursed heresy, which has clung to these infernal villages so long. Then the devil take your soul and body."

Bending over the bed, he spit in that wan face, and raised his hand as if to inflict a blow. A fierce glare passed over his features, which suddenly relaxed into a smile, as if some happy thought had suggested itself.

"Good," said he, aloud, "that will be a work of supererogation, and the blessed Bridget will intercede for me after this. I will—I will save her—I will baptize her into the true Church."

With these words he began to search about the room, and at last found some water, which he poured into a cup. Kneeling by the bedside, and making the sign of the cross, he chanted in a monotonous tone, *Baptizo te in nomine Domini, et Filii, et Spiritus Sancti. Amen.* Then making the sign of the cross on her forehead, he emptied the contents of the cup upon Marie's head.

The ignorance of the Franciscans was never more clearly demonstrated than by Malvicino's inability to perform a valid baptism. It may be doubted, however, whether Mr. Bramley-Moore was aware of the deficiencies in his account of the rite, although any child at a Catholic school would be able to point them out. Malvicino's other ministrations were equally defective. This is how he attended a dying soldier:—

The Abbot fell upon his knees, and began chanting the Litany for the dying. He dipped a feather into a phial of oil, and making the sign of the cross on Dugot's forehead, said: "Holy Mary, holy Abel, holy Abraham, all ye holy martyrs, St. Sylvester, St. Gregory, St. Augustine, St. Benedict, St. Francis, pray for him."

"There, Father Placido," said Malvicino, "I think we have shriven him, and may now attend to the wants of the flesh."

On another occasion, Iolande, who had been sent by "the council of ladies belonging to the Propaganda," to "go in among [the Waldenses], sow suspicions and jealousies," and "fan every element of discord," came to Malvicino, but declined to betray the secrets she had heard unless she previously obtained absolution. He said:—

"To make you happy, I will absolve you at once. By Pope Clement VII., who absolved Cellini from the blood of Bourbon, kneel down, and we will free you from the fault."

Iolande then knelt down before the Franciscan, who made the sign of the cross over her, and said: "*A Vinculis peccatorum nostrorum absolvat nos omnipotens et misericors Dominus.* Now, daughter, go on with your statement."

"Father, you have given me absolution, but can you give it to others who are concerned in the matter, except the heretics?"

"To be sure I can. Wasn't the absolution in the plural? By all the Popes in purgatory, and by all the Dominicans in hell," said the Franciscan, crossing himself, "we'd absolve them all, if the Church were only paid for it."

I must not devote too much space to Malvicino, but a few more of his original oaths must be quoted; if these were brought together they would form a long and striking litany. Here are samples:—

By Pope John XXII., who cursed the other seven Popes.

By the two right arms of John the Baptist at Genoa and Malta.

By Pope Innocent VI., who instituted the festival of the Holy Spear.

By the taxes of John XXII.

By the Cardinals who quarrelled for two years before they could elect a Pope.

By Pope Nicholas III., who declared the eggs which the Franciscans ate were not their property.

By Pope Urban VII., who was Pope for twelve days.

By Pope Gregory and his Propaganda.

By Pope Clement VIII. and his Congregation *De auxiliis.*

By all the Papal Bulls.

One feels that "By the piper that played before Moses" ought to have been added, to make the litany complete.

After a long career of crime, Malvicino approached his end. He had for a long time been girding at the Dominican Prior, Rorengo, chiefly with regard to the

Immaculate Conception. Rorengo had a "sepulchral frame, which appeared to have enjoyed a perpetual Lent since the day of his birth"—there is no pleasing these Protestants—and came upon Malvicino "engaged in plundering the dead," whereupon he ordered his arrest. "By the deposed Popes Gregory XII. and John XXIII., do you unfrock me so suddenly?" cried the Franciscan, "Let go my robe, or, by the Immaculate Virgin, I will add your bones to those I see bleaching yonder."

"Hideous immaculate, you swear upon what the Church has uttered no dogma. Are you immaculate yourself, or were you born in original sin?"

"How dare you, who are nothing more than a hooded Calvinist, or a Jansenist, arrest one who holds the Catholic faith respecting our Lady?"

"I tell you it is not a dogma, and never was," retorted Rorengo; "none but the impious Franciscans teach it, to curry favour with the ignorant."

"Hands off, you sepulchre worm, or I'll send you back to the grave from which you have been let out by accident. By all the rival Popes, I'll feed the ravens with you."

There was an awful struggle, during which "the word 'Immaculate' might be heard, mingled with imprecations to various Popes." Then they rolled over a precipice. Rorengo was killed, but Malvicino fell into a cleft. Here a raven picked out his eyes, and "the imprecation which the Abbot uttered against himself in Castelluzzo was fulfilled." He was then found by the Waldensians, became a Protestant, and died repentant. The book ends with the customary assurance—"Reader, our romance adheres in its main features to history."

The Oratorians, towards the end of the fifties, were bogeys in London. As a High Churchman, I was brought up to consider Roman Catholics with toleration and even with sympathy, but the Oratorians we regarded with aversion. Father Faber certainly in one instance unintentionally supplied Protestant minds with some justification for their view. I remember as a lad attending a Protestant lecture, in the course of which the following verse of an Oratorian hymn was quoted :—

> O what a way Saint Philip has got !
> He comes in the midst of your cares ;
> He passes you by, and turns back on the sly,
> And catches you unawares.

"Here," said the lecturer, "is the way they represent themselves!"

The Brompton Oratory was the scene of a remarkable story published in 1894 in *The Protestant Woman*, a monthly journal edited by Mrs. W. R. Arbuthnot, President of the W. P. U. (Women's Protestant Union), as well as of the Y. W. P. U. (for girls over fifteen), of the G. P. U. (for girls under fifteen), and of the B. P. U. (Boys' Protestant Union). The B. P. U. has evidently a great future in store for it : in the course of not much more than a year it enrolled "the noble number of sixty-seven boys," some of whom were at least eleven years old. Unfortunately, *The Protestant Woman* in which the narrative appeared is out of print, and I have mislaid my copy, so I am compelled to summarize from memory, and thus the narrative is deprived of much literary charm. The story in question—I quote from a letter by Mrs. Arbuthnot herself—"was communicated by Miss Clara Lowe: she knew all the parties mentioned, and was anxious that her name should appear at the end of the article," which it did. No one reading the story can fail to estimate Miss Lowe's veracity.

The narrator was a member of the Oratory congregation, and went one Sunday afternoon to a prayer-meeting at St. James's Hall. She at once saw the errors of Popery, and acquainted her confessor with the fact. That night she saw from her room at the top of an adjoining house that service for the dead was being performed in the Oratory, and she knew that it was for herself, who was regarded as spiritually dead. Her confessor came to see her, but she would not let him in. So they arranged a meeting in Westminster Abbey, where they walked up and down and talked for an hour or two. But the lady was true to her convictions.

Just about this time the Superior of the Oratory died, and it leaked out that he had turned Protestant. The priests did their best to prevent its being known, but known it was, though the poor man—I suppose it was Father Faber—was buried with all Catholic rites. The story received unexpected confirmation, for once, when a captain (whose name I forget) was narrating it at a meeting in the South of England —I fancy it was at Southampton—a gentleman in the audience rose and said he could testify to its truth, as he had been cook at the Oratory at the time. So there can be no doubt about it.

The Protestant Woman is great at stories of this kind. The number for October, 1895, contains one entitled "The Adventures of a Romish Priest," of which the following is an abridgment:—

Father B—— was the zealous priest of a small village in Belgium. To him the Bible was an unknown book, but

Priests. 75

he *believed* it to be full of blasphemies of the vilest character. One day some tourists passing through the parish distributed some small, well-bound Testaments to his parishioners. On the following Sunday, in his sermon, he commanded all the faithful to bring the heretical books to him to be burnt, threatening with excommunication those who refused to give them up. A few hid their newly found treasure, but many obeyed the priest's mandate. But, strange to say, in God's over-ruling providence, the *binding* of the books so pleased Father B——, that he could not bring himself to burn anything so good and pretty, and so superior to much foreign binding. For a long time the contents were unheeded, but at last with fear and trembling the priest ventured to open one, and though he searched diligently he could find none of those wicked things he so firmly believed were contained in the pages of the New Testament.

One feels sorry for Father B——'s disappointment.

The next thing that struck him was that a priest's blessing the water was absolutely useless.

It had been his custom on a certain day to bless a large tub of water, and people came from miles distant with bottles and jugs in which to carry away the blessed fluid with which to sprinkle their barns and granaries as a preservative against rats and mice.

But when they came, " Father B—— told them to go home and get some good cats," and this annoyed his congregation, to whose conservative instincts the idea seems to have appeared new and revolutionary. Then Father B—— went to Antwerp, to consult a Protestant Pastor. But no sooner had he rung the door-bell, than he was

horrified at the thought of the deadly sin he was about to commit in holding intercourse with a heretic; he took to his heels and ran away as fast as his legs would carry him. After a time he made a second attempt, and this time he was shown into the only sitting-room of the very poor pastor. There, horror of horrors, he saw a baby in a cradle! The sin of marriage in an ordained priest being thus forcibly brought home to him, he says in his manuscript autobiography (for private circulation only) that he spent nearly all his time in arguing on this one point only.

One would like to know how Father B—— came to regard the pastor as "an ordained priest," but still more would it be a joy to behold "his manuscript autobiography."

Then he went back to his parish, where

his simple preaching of the Gospel attracted the attention of neighbouring priests, who reported his heresies to the bishop of the diocese. For some reason the bishop appeared extremely anxious not to proceed to extremities with Father B——. On the contrary, he invited him to make a fortnight's retreat in a celebrated monastery, where he might confer with his brethren on the needed "reforms," and give himself, with them, to prayer and meditation on the subject. The invitation was readily accepted by the guileless priest, but, though treated with the utmost courtesy and allowed a certain amount of liberty within the walls of the monastery, excuses were made for not allowing him to leave it, and he soon made the unwelcome discovery that he had fallen into a trap, and was in reality a close prisoner. His letters were intercepted, and no tidings reached him from the outer world. Concealing his amazement, he did indeed "meditate," but it was on the best method of effecting his escape from his unlooked for and most unwelcome position. The monastery was surrounded by a wall eighteen feet in height, well covered with carefully pruned fruit-trees. One day, when walking in the garden, he noticed a remarkable high ladder against the wall, and then and there he made a secret resolution that if the ladder should be left all night, God helping him, he would leap from the wall at midnight and be once more a free man.

Here one pauses to reflect on the providential stupidity which left "a remarkably high ladder against the wall" of a prison.

A blessing rested on his daring enterprise. He alighted on the outside of the wall in perfect safety, and once more, as before in Antwerp, he ran as fast as his legs would carry him, never once stopping till he had put six miles between himself and the monastic prison.

After this only one course remained open to him.

From that time he ceased to hope for "reforms" in the Romish Church, but he came out boldly as an Evangelical preacher in the Free Church in Belgium. No longer a celibate, he rejoices in the society of a devoted wife, and the sight of an innocent babe in a cradle in the sitting-room of a parsonage no longer fills his soul with pious horror!

Hildebrand and the Emperor, by the Rev. Joseph Sortain, A.B.,[1] is another Protestant novel in which "the facts and suggestions of History" are "most conscientiously observed." Ranulph, an "earnestly affectionate and evidently ingenuous priest," was married to Elgitha, " a young and beautiful female," and the story opens in " the room [apparently there was only one] of a castle some few miles from Spires," furnished with such accessories as "rich oak panels on the walls, rude but impressive paintings, and Venetian mirrors." "It was in the autumn of the year of our Lord 1076," and the edict of the Pope regarding the marriage of the clergy had just been promulgated. The Pope was then living in a small room at Vercelli, the only furniture of which seems to have been "a triple crown which lay upon a velvet cushion, together with a massive gold crosier," and a "reverend secretary, who stood with his arms crossed and with his head bent, as if in the presence of a divinity." Hildebrand "wore a countenance of com-

[1] Second edition, revised. Longmans, 1851.

mand, intelligence, and conscious power, such as eclipsed the comparative meanness of the chamber."

When the Countess Matilda came to see him, the Pope said, "Whosoever cometh I will in nowise cast out. Admit her instantly." So in she came, and, "although there was a crown on her fair head, knelt devoutly at the Pontiff's feet," who, in his turn, "blessed the royal suppliant with unwonted vivacity." But he assumed a different attitude when Henry IV. went to Canossa. "Even Matilda, soul-subjected as she was, shuddered" when Hildebrand, "with malignant glee," observed, "Pride goeth before destruction, and a haughty spirit before a fall": the "few sleek, sycophantic ecclesiastics" who "smiled assent," "grew the paler as they did so"; and when Matilda put in a word for Henry, the Pope, "opening a vellum missal, said, 'Silence! I command thee! or I will excommunicate thee also.'" Henry said "*Miserere, Domine!*" through several pages, and at last the Pope relented. The Abbot of Clugny said Mass, while the Pope "seated himself beside the altar, listened to and observed the service"—just as if he were an "aggrieved parishioner" in a ritualistic church—and "partook of the sacrament alone." When Ranulph came to see him, Hildebrand addressed him in "a tone low and deep, far more terrible than the recent high one"; "it was soul-thrilling to catch the sound of his grating teeth, and his ever-terrific eyes glared with an unwonted fierceness." He ordered Ranulph's tongue to be torn out, but this seems not to have been done, for he talked up to the moment of his death, which took place in Winchester, and his ghost spoke nearly a page when it visited Hildebrand later on.

Priests. 79

Another picture of a priest who was ultimately converted is furnished by a delightful book called *Falconbridge;* "a Tale of Old, in the Times of Henry VIII. : by Mistress Alice."[1] "The desire to do good, and to contribute to the comfort of others, is the chief object of the writer in presenting these pages to the public. Read me, and Report me, is all the Author asks." I have complied with the first request, and now proceed to carry out the second.

The youthful Father Leonard [he seems to have had no surname] had just been appointed confessor in the ancient family of Melrose, consisting of Sir Felton Melrose, his lady, three sons, and two daughters. . . . At eighteen, Leonard found himself inducted into the priesthood, under the renunciation of the world, of all domestic ties, and taking vows, denying to man what God had allowed, making a Church machine of a fine noble character; but Leonard had this yet to learn. Seven years he spent in a monastry [sic]. The poor and the sick were alike visited, the young married, infants baptized, and the dead interred. Schools also, to a limited extent, came under his notice in the monastry.

Leonard's monastic training seems to have taken place before he was "inducted into the priesthood." The Melrose family were quite nice people—they "moved in the usual routine of daily duties observed at that time; there was much family love, tempering the over-restraint of the period." Father Leonard added "tutorial" to his "professional duties" : "study for the youths and embroidery for the maidens, beguiled the lagging hours. . . . Weeks were succeeded by months; still thus went on every-day life, leaving as little stain on time, by actual commission of evil,

[1] Hamilton, Adams & Co. Preface dated 1870.

as they left little impression on the higher demands of the immortal creature."[1]

Father Leonard had a "more open view" of his religious duties, attributable to "his not having been so shackled as the strictly monastic orders." Moreover the Melroses, like the people in Mr. W. S. Gilbert's ballad of "Gentle Alice Brown," had "nothing to confess," they were "so ridiculously good"; so that the priest had "little to do in enacting penances." When, therefore, "Maude mentioned her desire to be confessed, lamenting that too long a period had passed since this rite of the Church had been observed,"

the colour mounted into the Father's cheek, as he replied: "Daughter, the routine of daily life at Falconbridge is of so even a tenor, so little from without to distract the mind, and so much within of active duties to engage and employ aright, that I have not enjoined as frequent confession as the Church might enforce; but after evening vespers [2] I will await you at the Confessional."

"The shadows had cast their gentle gloom over the interior of the chapel, aided by the richly painted windows, called in more recent days, 'The dim

---

[1] One feels inclined to echo the sentiments of Alice on hearing *Jabberwocky*: "It seems very pretty, but it's *rather* hard to understand. Somehow it seems to fill my head with ideas, only I don't know exactly what they are."

[2] This specification of the time of vespers was necessary, because "morning vespers" formed part of the daily "routine" at Falconbridge. This is a pleasant variation on the "evening Mass" which frequently occurs in Protestant fiction. It is in the evening that, in Spanish monasteries, "mass for the dead is performed with all its accompanying ceremonial of incense and requiems" (*St. Mary's Convent*, Partridge). The Oratorian custom is to have High Mass late in the afternoon: "Lanty had intended to spend his first unemployed afternoon in a visit to the South Kensington Museum, ending up with attendance at a special High Mass at the Brompton Oratory" (*Temple Bar*, April, 1897, p. 577).

religious light.' Father Leonard was seated in the Confessional, when a light step was heard." This was Maude, who made her confession, and received the following admonition and absolution :—

"Daughter, a sin that causes you such real grief, so truthfully declared, we doubt not will be watched and prayed against; penance, however, the Church declares needful. I leave you, therefore, as the best judge, to exercise that self-denial and self-constraint that may overcome the evil, absolving you from the punishment due to your sin, and praying that superior strength may be vouchsafed you!"

Father Leonard's room

was fitted up (the sleeping apartment within), as we might suppose, with a small altar, upon which stood a crucifix, rather rudely carved, and other sacred relics. In remoter parts of the room were manuscripts on shelves, more than in those monkish days might have been found in a monastry. There was, indeed, the only one wanting, that could lead into all truth!

He was "not a Jesuit, be it remembered, but a true son of England, who had not been tutored in the knowledge of all evil, in order that he might resist it." When he came across Mr. Lascells, "a man of acute mind and ready perception," he found a kindred spirit. Leonard's "candid bearing and well-timed remarks" impressed Lascells, who was a frequent visitor at Falconbridge, very favourably. They became fast friends, and Leonard spent much time at Drayton House, "returning to the Manor for closing vespers."

When abroad, Lascells had been gravely dissatisfied with the Church to which he still nominally belonged; he "had discerned, with his clear eye, that many abuses were allowed to exist." He confided his views to Leonard, and took him to a ruined convent, where, in the underground cells, he touched a secret spring, and disclosed a "human skeleton resting against the wall, immured evidently for some alleged crime, and that, too, in the midst of life—bricked up within its living grave!" Then Lascells introduced Leonard to the torture-chamber, where, with regrettable carelessness, several instruments of torture were "lying on the floor." The room was dark, but

artificial light would reveal fully what passed the speechless accused, the dim, cold eye of the accuser, or the flashing one of the detector who had secured his victim, while cowled monk and veiled abbess listened to all that passed.

Leonard's "soul sank within him," although "he knew full well that such had been the practice of his Church, if man or woman, monk or nun, infringed the sacredness of their vows"; and they left the room. Passing through the gallery,

Leonard observed that the walls had been covered with grotesque colours and figures innumerable, of which but few remained; still there was sufficient to show that these figures were floating in the flames of Purgatory. We therefore judge that the nuns, whenever passing in or out of their cells, had to look upon the agonies of the condemned souls in flames of fire. Was it not enough to shut them up from the face of the living, without shutting them up to the contemplation of those, the ever dying but never dead?

As they rode home, Lascells told Leonard the history of his sister, who became a Lady Abbess, preluding his narrative by quoting the lines

"O call my brother back to me":

it is clear that Mrs. Hemans, to whom they have

usually been attributed, must have taken them (unacknowledged) from an earlier writer, as the incidents narrated occurred in the reign of Henry VIII.

Would that space would allow me to quote the conversation of this charming couple! Two sentences must suffice:—

"It has been much in your favour, my young friend [it is Mr. Lascells who speaks], having been educated for a specific branch of the Church, which placed you, at an early age, tutor and domestic priest in a family so well ordered, as that of my old and dear friend, Sir Felton Melrose. The little demand made for the exercise of your unbounded authority, permitted it to slumber and grow torpid, while an energetic mind was preparing to judge for itself, of all those different phases of society, and how far they were acting out the religious principles of the Church."

"You are, perhaps, correct, Mr. Lascells, in this supposition, still, my conflict was great, and all the penance and all the mortification used, only showed me still further its powerlessness to give any peace to a tried conscience. Scale by scale dropped from my eyes; unsupported, untaught by any human being, I found the whole system begin to totter, and felt that I should be crushed under its ruins!"

Towards the middle of the book, Sir Felton and his sons go to town. Roland was "approved at the War Office," and the family were charmed with "the stately Tower, the Monument [!], St. Paul's, and the bridges [!] thrown over the Thames." Meanwhile, Lascells and Leonard went abroad, and had a terrible time of it. Leonard went to a Jesuit University, country not stated, where he was

greatly struck with the very limited view [the pupils] were allowed of English history. They were better acquainted with the rest of Europe; and Italy as the centre of Papal supremacy, they enthusiastically admired. The German nation were condemned as heretics, and Bohemia also.

Spain and Portugal elicited their Gallican approval; but France, with its fallen Church, was suspected.

After imprisonments and various perils, he made his way to Hamburg, where he narrated to Lascells his adventures, concluding with an announcement that he was no more "Father" Leonard but a layman. Then a Dutch gentleman gave him a Bible; he was introduced to William Tyndal, and, having fallen in love with Bertha St. Quentin, consulted him on his course of action :—

"In my own particular case," said Leonard, "you would not consider marriage objectionable?"

"By no means," was Master Tyndal's reply. "Having renounced Romanism altogether, you are now to be judged of as a Protestant; and happily we have no such customs."

"There comes a sound of marriage-bells," and the story ends.

All priests, however, are not so fortunate. Probably "the confessor," whose "diary" is given in *London Homes*—a work by Catherine Sinclair, author of *Beatrice*—never saw the error of his ways. Here are some extracts from the work, which speak for themselves, and give a vivid picture of the daily routine of a priest's life :—

Lay wide awake all night on the floor, and hope soon entirely to conquer sleep. Prostrate on the bare stones, I told my beads over incessantly before the image of my patron, St. Dunstan. . . .

Have refrained entirely all this month from washing or shaving. Put on my usual hair-shirt and the belt with spikes through the breast. Scourged myself severely, remained silently looking at the wall during three hours, and ate no breakfast. . . .

After I showed Lady Penzance the beautiful little picture

for our Chapel of "the Mater Dolorosa," she asked, with a look of stupid astonishment, why we represent the Virgin Mary wearing a crown of thorns [!] ...

That obstinate heretic, Colonel Dermonville, seeing that Lady Mary has a taste for excitement, has been travelling her about all over the Continent to keep her away from Romanists [!] ...

Visited my school. The children had been for some days, as I desired, sitting with their eyes fixed on a whitewashed wall, therefore now they are ready to believe anything. Shall get up a few visions next week, and exhibit a bleeding picture, which is easily managed by fixing behind the canvas some leeches saturated with blood, from the hospitals. ... Enjoined a total fast on the children to-morrow. ...

Sir Joseph is almost at disinheriting pitch in favour of our Church, for I refuse him absolution if he leaves more than a shilling to those heretics his son. ...

Finding her questions often difficult to answer, I have enjoined [Lady Penzance] to take a vow of silence, for unless her mind be put to sleep, it may turn out, as our Cardinal said, that "every one trusted with a Bible becomes a Protestant." ...

Six Irish reapers came to confession. Ordered them to spend all Wednesday on bare knees at the Holy Well of St. Bridget, telling their beads, and to fast till sunset. ...

I have half promised Lady Mary that she shall at last be canonized, so her vain and ambitious spirit will be in full work to gain this distinction, and she shall soon exceed any *Faquir* in the desert for filth and starvation. ...

I trust the day is not far distant when there shall be no homes in England, but the men all living in monasteries, the women in convents, and only the priests at liberty. We shall then have all the broad lands of Britain for Church property, and unbounded incomes to the priesthood, with power that no one shall question.

I have advised [Lady Mary] to try some innocent amusements, such as the girls enjoy at our Retreat, to make a procession with her maid and nursery-governess round the house, to string arbutus berries for a cross, to have up the kitten and the Skye terrier, to embroider an apron for

St. Bridget, to weave a garland of snowdrops for St. Theresa, and to try how many times in a day she can count over her beads.

[Pope Joan's] real name was Gilberta, but she took the name of John English when delivering public lectures, and became unanimously elected Pope John VIII.

The "penny stories," from which I have already quoted in my chapter on Nuns, introduce us to priests of other lands. In *The Boy Martyr, a Story of the Inquisition*,[1] for example, we become acquainted with Father Doria, "a proud, unbending priest, utterly devoid of feeling, inveterate in his hatred against all heretics, [who] spared neither pains nor trouble to bring any such under the notice of the deservedly dreaded Inquisition."

During the reign of Pope Pius V., in the year 1567, there lived in a beautiful mansion not far from Naples a wealthy and noble Italian called Victor de Manfresti, who, while holding a high command in the army of "His Holiness," and striving with all his power to maintain the honour of the Romish Church, still scarcely approved of that merciless persecution of the Protestants which at this period had become universal, and characterized by such revolting and hideous cruelties, especially throughout Italy and Spain.

Manfresti, to whom Father Doria was confessor, had adopted a little boy named Guilo (*sic*), who had "in the wide world no relative but his grandmother." Guilo had obtained a New Testament, which he read when he ought to have been attending to his master, and the latter was not unnaturally annoyed at this neglect of his duties. After supper, instead of going to bed, Guilo made his way to his grandmother, whose name was Mariano (!), and who entertained as a guest

[1] Shaw's Penny Series, No. 6.

"Alberto the Protestant." "Long and late that night Guilo remained in the little cottage listening earnestly to the words of life uttered by Alberto."

After a time Mariano died, and Guilo, who was attending her, "sank into a deep sound slumber," owing, it would seem—although the suggestion of the narrator is hardly reverent—to his perusal of the New Testament.

Twelve o'clock came, and suddenly the door, which Guilo had not thought to fasten, was pushed noiselessly open, and a tall man, enveloped in the folds of a long dark cloak, entered softly. He threw back the hood of his cloak, revealing in the action the harsh features of the priest, Father Doria. Guilo, his long dark hair thrown back off his forehead, was lying with the Testament still open in his hand; but so deep was his sleep that he neither saw nor heard the entrance of Father Doria. Astonishment, mingled with hate and anger, contracted the priest's dark brow as he gazed upon the prostrate form. Grimly he smiled. One glance had been enough to assure him that Mariano was beyond his reach; but the boy Guilo could not escape, and dearly he determined should his temerity cost him. He bent silently over the child, and gently, without rousing him, took the Testament from his hand; then, drawing the cowl over his head, crept in the same stealthy way from the cottage, carefully closing the door as he passed out.

The next day "a lackey in a handsome livery informed Guilo that Father Doria desired his immediate presence in the shrubbery." The interview was not a pleasant one, and must have been rendered more striking from the fact that during it, as we learn from the accompanying pictures, the priest entirely changed his costume—a circumstance not mentioned in the text. Father Doria tore the Testament "in several pieces, and flung them [all except one, which he kept to show to Manfresti] at Guilo's feet." Then he called him, "Accursed boy!" and struck him across the shoulders and upon the forehead with a heavy cane. But Guilo remained firm, and confessed his faith, which, as one might except, largely consisted of negations.

"I avow my faith in the Reformed religion and I am ready to suffer for the sake of that Saviour who died for me upon the Cross. I do not believe in any other power to save me but that of Jesus Christ. I do not believe that the Virgin Mary, or the saints, or the intercession of man, have anything to do with my salvation."

Then the priest said: "Out of my presence, accursed heretic!" and proceeded to acquaint Manfresti with the fact that he had nourished a viper in his household. The noble Italian begged that the boy might be spared; but in vain: "that night strong men came and bore Guilo away from Belli-doni," and confined him in a dungeon of the Inquisition. Here are introduced two ancient blocks representing the tortures of the Inquisition, chiefly remarkable for the absence of any one who could possibly represent Guilo. Father Doria brought Father Felio, but Guilo's faith remained unshaken. Manfresti, by means of a heavy bribe, secured admission to the prison; but even his efforts were vain, and Guilo, having bequeathed some papers which he had hidden under a stone to his beloved master, died of his sufferings.

The sequel may be guessed.

In the palace of Belli-doni three days after this Manfresti sits reading the papers he had found under the stone. His face wears a fixed, determined expression. The door opens, and Father Doria enters. He has come to demand the promised purse of gold.

Manfresti rises. There is a calm majestic dignity in his bearing, as he folds his arms and exclaims,—
"Priest, you may take all; I am a Protestant."

. . . .

Not all the influence and power of Manfresti can save him from the tyranny and might of the Inquisition.
A few weeks after he is burnt as a heretic at the stake.

I have a large number of stories like this, but I must not weary my readers. As an example of the foulness of which a certain type of Protestant is not ashamed, I will mention *By-and-by*, "A Thrilling Tale, Deeply Interesting to every Britisher who loveth Britain," which is published by Mr. John Kensit. This is an outrage upon decency, and I am therefore precluded from quoting from it; but no sketch of Protestant fiction would be complete if all reference to this class of literature were omitted. It is one of the saddest features of this kind of controversy that it does not hesitate to put into circulation books, the public sale of which has been described by an impartial critic as "unquestionably an outrage on public decency, [while] the indiscriminate circulation of such literature must be necessarily injurious to public morals."[1] With this description I leave so unsavoury a subject.

It must not be supposed that Protestant fiction concerning priests is confined to stories; it appears also in tracts and leaflets. Here, for example, is a small four-page tract, issued by the Religious Tract Society, called "Where Father Anthony came Short," written by a well-known clergyman of the Church of England, the Rev. P. B. Power, M.A.

[1] *Truth*, August 29, 1889, where Mr. Kensit's publications are forcibly dealt with.

Father Anthony was the Romish Priest who had charge of what one might almost call one of the Irish settlements in London. Being a foreigner he did not speak English very fluently, and did not understand much Irish. Amongst his flock Father Anthony had an old woman named Mrs. Bourke.

An Irish-speaking city missionary paid her a visit one day, and during his stay told her the plain and simple way of salvation throught the merits and all-sufficient sacrifice of Jesus Christ offered once for all.

But poor Mrs. Bourke had a sore trouble on her mind which hindered her from receiving this blessed message as her friend desired. And Father Anthony was the cause of her trouble.

"Oh, sir," said she, "there is one thing that troubles me day and night; I fear that my sins are not forgiven me, as Father Anthony did not understand what I revealed to him in my last confession. I spoke to him in Irish, and he did not understand me. Although he listened to me and received my money[1] yet I never had the satisfaction to know whether my sins were forgiven or not."

"And," said Mrs. Bourke's visitor, "do you really believe that the priests have the power to forgive sins?"

"Well indeed," said she, "I cannot tell for a certainty, but it is an old saying that the priests have power to forgive sins; you know that they claim such power in Ireland. God help me! I am now upwards of seventy-four years of age, and what will become of me if I am left in the fires of purgatory? I have got no money to pay for masses to release my poor soul."

Father Anthony, "being a foreigner," might be excused for "not understanding much Irish"—the wonder is that he understood any—but here we have a clergyman of the same Church as "Father" Stanton

---

[1] I am glad to say that my representations to the Religious Tract Society have resulted in the omission of the words "and received my money" from the latest reprint of this tract; and the editor of the series expresses his conviction that "all that was intended was that she gave him a thank-offering." The rest of the tract, however, still remains as I have quoted it.

and "Father" Dolling, so ignorant and so wicked as to represent a priest taking money for absolution, although he did not even understand the confession of his penitent; while Mrs. Bourke, though going to confession and paying for it, could not tell whether in England the priests claimed to forgive sins!

Probably no lie has been more assiduously propagated than this of paying for absolution. It is a gratifying evidence of the spread of truth, that this article of the Protestant creed is disappearing; I fancy it may come to be regarded as a Catholic figment, for Mr. C. H. Collette, in his Protestant Alliance pamphlet, *Is it Honest?* says, with astonishing effrontery: " I deny than any such assertion is made by Protestants, and demand proofs." This demand can easily be gratified: here is an extract from a recent work which was recommended by the editor of *Life and Light* as "a thoroughly good Protestant book." A young Catholic girl says:—

"Genie and I can do all these things that we like, and then go to confession and get our minds settled up, and take communion as pure as new-born babies. I *have* thought it rather hard on Bridget, and that kind of folk, who have little money and so much to pay that they can hardly buy a pair of shoes; but the *money* makes no difference to us, for mother's purse is always full." [1]

In *Saved for Nothing*, "a Tale for the Young," [2] we are told of a woman who, "being seized with remorse for a life spent in fearful wickedness," went to confession.

---
[1] *Almost a Nun*, p. 78.
[2] This story, although recent, is out of print, and it is fair to say that Mr. W. B. Horner, the publisher, does not propose to re-issue it.

The priest pronounced the sentence—it was this: "A large sum of money is required by the Church for alms before such sin can be forgiven." These sinful men call themselves the "church," and pretend that God has given them power to forgive sins! The poor woman answered, "I have no money, my father." "Then you cannot have absolution," replied the priest. "I am too poor ever to gain such a sum." "You cannot be absolved any other way," said the Romish priest. With a heavy, burdened soul, poor Catherine went to another and another priest, but each gave her a similar answer.

Should Mr. Collette "demand" further "proofs," there will be no difficulty in supplying them. It is, however, gratifying that he should be ashamed of even one of the fictions which the party that he represents so persistently circulates, and emboldens one to hope that the same creditable feeling may be manifested with regard to other Protestant calumnies.

One or two earlier examples of this class of Protestant fiction may be quoted. "Charlotte Elizabeth"—of whom we shall hear later—tells us of a young man,

a most extravagant and dissipated character, who had, through his own vicious conduct, forfeited every advantage that he acquired. Still, being "a good Catholic," all was right with him: and the sins for which, with sixpence, he could any day purchase absolution, never gave him a moment's concern.[1]

Miss Sinclair makes the landlord of a low lodging-house say:—

The Irish priest comes here once a week to absolve my people; and the only crime for which there can be no absolution is, if they have not prepared money to pay for his blessing. A man steals a purse, and if he gives half the money to Father O'Shaughnessy for absolution, he keeps

[1] *Chapters on Flowers*, chap. xv.

possession of the other half with a safe conscience, and drinks himself drunk for the rest of the week. Gin and Popery are the two expenses that ruin them all.[1]

Father O'Shaughnessy reminds me that I have said little about the Irish priest of Protestant fiction. This is not because he plays an insignificant part in it, but rather on account of his ubiquity. Father Murphy, of the "House Without a Name," to whom I referred in my chapter on "Nuns and Convents," may be taken as a type; and his almost-namesake, Father O'Murphy, otherwise known as "the Star of Maynooth," is an example of the Irish priest at home, where he went about "followed by a drove of armed reapers, in corduroys, unbuttoned at the knees, drab frieze coats, blackthorn cudgels, ready for any row, and a wisp of straw round their waists."[2]

The *Stirling Tracts* furnish notable examples of Protestant fiction. Here is one on "The Holy Trade in Masses"—which is, by the way, noteworthy in that the priest is described as "kind." He certainly was obliging, even to excess—I wonder what his bishop thought of him, for we are told that, "did a parishioner want a dispensation, a dispensation was granted him." Some of his parishioners wanted Masses for fine weather, others for rain, and the priest promised to obtain both. The millers, who wanted water to turn their mills, came to the priest, and their interview concluded thus :—[3]

We are come to ask you for a few masses.
Very well.—And you will make it rain?

[1] *London Homes*, p. 61.
[2] *Op. cit.* "Lady Mary Pierrepont," p. 15.
[3] Here, as throughout these papers, I print the extracts exactly as given in the tract quoted, not altering punctuation or any other detail.

I hope so.—Enough to turn the mill?—As much as possible.

Without delay?—I will say the mass to-morrow.

All right. Here is——

How much?—Nothing at all—I was going to say—here is what we had thought, the more it rains the more we will pay!

No, no; that is against the canons of the Church. Pay beforehand: never afterwards. I prefer giving it to you pretty cheap: four masses for eight shillings. If it were for fair weather, good; but we only ask you for rain.

The millers, seeing his reverence thoroughly resolute, drew the money from their pockets, with as much difficulty as if it were stuck to the bottom, and his reverence put down his receipts in an account-book as follows:

Received this day to obtain sunshine as soon as possible, £0 8 0
Ditto ditto to obtain rain at the same time 0 8 0

Then came "a fine lady with tossing feathers," who wanted a dispensation for her maid, who desired to marry a Protestant. After some talk, the priest said:—

A dispensation from the Pope must be had.—That is exactly what I come for. What will the expense of it be?

Here the priest took time to reflect; he mentally ran over the lady's toilet, from head to foot; cast a look through the window to judge of the carriage, and, when his calculation was made, he said, Five pounds.—Five pounds!

Yes, madam; I must write, and wait to receive the answer, and the documents. All that—— Surely, but one word frightens me; wait, did you say? Now that is most troublesome.

Forty days are required.—In that case we can think no more about it; if nothing was needed but money——

To tell the truth, money might indeed hasten the proceedings, and then——Hasten them, then; Bridget is to be married in a week.

Well, then, it will be eight pounds.—It is expensive work, but no matter, I agree to it. Here are eight sovereigns. The wedding this day week in your church.

Then came the intended husband, who declined to pay for a dispensation, and said his future wife would turn Protestant if the priest insisted on payment, adding :—

And now, take your choice, either to marry us for nothing, or not at all.

If it were not to avoid scandal, I would refuse you.—As you please.

When are you to be married?—In a week.

Very well; come and remind me the day before. I will marry you without a dispensation; but put down ten shillings for the expenses of the ceremony.—Ah, your reverence, I thought myself pretty sharp; but I acknowledge that you bear the bell—here are ten shillings.

That's right. Away with you.—Directly, your reverence, and with pleasure!

The countryman went out. The priest, in a bad humour, took up his account-book again, and wrote :—

Received this day for a marriage with a Protestant, £8 0 0
Ditto   ditto   ditto   ditto,   0 10 0

The young man left behind him a tract, which the priest read, and then "took down a Bible"—surely his possession of such a book was exceptional!—and verified the quotations the tract contained.

His mind seemed rent in twain; sometimes he stamped on the floor, at others he raised his eyes to heaven. At length he again opened the Bible, and his eyes fell upon these words :—"What is a man profited, if he shall gain the whole world, and lose his own soul?" Matt. xvi. 26. "Pardon, Lord, pardon!" cried he at last, and pushing away the gold which was upon the table, he eagerly seized the Bible, pressed it against his heart, and, for some moments, allowed his tears to flow in silence upon the Sacred Volume.

Some days later, a girl, for whose private intention he had said Mass, came to thank him.

Said I to myself, I wish some bad luck might happen to Bridget; I will have a mass said for that! And there she falls into the water! Oh! I did not push her in! God did it himself alone, by means of your masses!

Wicked girl!—But, your reverence, you helped me.

I was not aware of your wish.—But you told me that the mass would succeed all the same.

This was more than the priest could stand.

He understood that his church and mass were accomplices in this terrible doctrine; and seizing his missal from off the table, he said to the girl:—"My child, I have deceived you, or rather, I have deceived myself. The mass is an error, I will never say it again. It was my livelihood, but my soul was near being lost by such a livelihood! I prefer burning my book to burning myself!" And saying this he threw the missal into the fire.

Farewell, my child, said he at last; be sure that a mass that can be sung to obtain sun and rain at the same time, a mass that can be said in favour of a wish unknown—a homicide wish, that mass cannot be commanded by God!

May God forgive me for all those I have said.

After this he became a Protestant.

One conviction will be forced upon all who read such tissues of absurdity as the two narratives last quoted—it is that, by some strange accident, a verse must have been omitted from the Bible of those who write these fictions. The verse is the sixteenth of the twentieth chapter of Exodus, and runs: " Thou shalt not bear false witness against thy neighbour."

IV. THE LAITY.

"LIKE priest, like people," is an old proverb, but it is hardly true of Catholic clergy and laity as depicted in Protestant fiction. Speaking generally, the former are crafty, clever, plausible beings, whose object, in which they are usually successful, is to keep their people in ignorance. The laity, indeed, occasionally escape from their thrall, but in such cases they generally become Protestants. Miss Catherine Sinclair tells us that Cardinal Wiseman said: "Every one trusted with a Bible becomes a Protestant."[1] It would be disrespectful to so high an authority to ask for a reference to the place where his Eminence published this opinion; moreover Protestant writers are not strong in references. The mere hearing of any passage in the Bible is often sufficient to ensure conversion: when Catherine (not Miss Sinclair, but the heroine of the little story I quoted at length in the last chapter) "heard the good clergyman read the Bible at family prayers," "she found out that the priests had taught her wrong when she was a child."[2] The "shrewd and quick-reasoning mind" of Pat, the hero of *Sheltering Arms*[3]—who, like Catherine and other characters of Protestant fiction, seems to have had no surname—when he heard for the first time that our Lord took children in His arms and blessed them, was "especially impressed" by "one incident in this narrative"—"it was that those who stood

[1] *London Homes: The Priest and the Curate*, p. 17.
[2] *Near Home*. Sixty-eighth thousand (1873), p. 130.
[3] By M. E. Clements. Nelson & Sons, 1885.

around Jesus, saints though they were, had bidden the mothers to keep their little children away, and that Jesus Himself, not Mary His mother, had taken them in His arms."[1] Pat had been taught "that our Saviour is too great, too high, too holy for sinners to come to Him in prayer, but that Mary, who is with Him in heaven, is good and pitiful, and that she can hear their prayers, and that she will plead with Him to have mercy on them."[2] There is no need to multiply instances of this result of Bible-reading.[3] Yet it may be noted that some 55,000 copies of a sixpenny New Testament, recommended by numerous cardinals and bishops, have been sold in little more than ten years; while, such is Popish perversity! in spite of Cardinal Wiseman's dictum, the number of conversions to Protestantism has not been conspicuous.

I propose in this chapter to deal first with those "born Catholics," and then to say something about converts.

Born Catholics in Protestant fiction, especially if they happen to be Irish, are, for the most part, characterized by ignorance and stupidity. The ignorance of the Irish naturally impresses the nation which first prevented them from obtaining education, save at the loss of their faith, and has ever since blamed them for the want of it. But in Scotland Catholics are not much better.

The inhabitants of Clanmarina, "a village on the west border of Inverness-shire," figured in my second chapter. It will be remembered that Father Eustace

---

[1] P. 41. [2] P. 20.
[3] It is set forth at length in *The Light of the Gospel*. Partridge & Co. 1d.

"impoverished the poorest by his commanding extortions." "Their wretchedness," we are further told,[1] "exhibited a perfect exaggeration of Irish misery in its most priest-ridden districts," and they themselves, so Lord Eaglescairn, their landlord, said—and who would ask for a more impartial witness?—were "the most good-for-nothing idlers in the kingdom."

The Earl of Eaglescairn [was] a Roman Catholic peer, . . . proud, cold and obstinate, his immense fortune seemed as naturally and irresponsibly his own as a leopard might consider the spots on his skin, or a peacock the feathers on his tail. [He] considered all the small tenantry as his goods and chattels, to be disposed of at his own pleasure, and [cared] not a farthing about the condition of his kilted clan, or about the condition of any mortal but himself. . . . He piqued himself on some blundering knowledge of foreign affairs, while in utter ignorance of his own, and had a sort of heavy eloquence, mouthing and sententious, in which he delayed a final division [in the House of Lords] on many a question, of which he in no degree influenced the actual decision.

Lord Eaglescairn had two sons. The younger he "treated as a poor dependant forced on his bounty," so Tom joined the 93rd Highlanders, and while at Gibraltar ran off "from the very gates of the nunnery of St. Bridget with a beautiful Spanish girl, on the very evening when she was to have been forced to take the veil. . . . In consequence of her wishing to become a Protestant, the young bride had undergone unheard-of hardships from her bigoted family, in order to make her consent that, while yet in the bloom of her youth, she should become immured for life in a silent and solitary cell within the convent of St. Bridget." Lord Eaglescairn thereupon "consigned the young couple to oblivion, such as the living are

[1] *Beatrice*, ch. i.

sometimes more condemned to by their relatives than even the dead," and they "retreated from the persecutions of Popish and Spanish relatives into the cool depths of retirement," where they were converted to "enlightened Protestantism." Then Tom died, and his wife (whose conversion seems to have been but temporary) "retired inconsolable to the convent of St. Bridget."

The death of his heir, Lord Iona, coupled with the fact of his "having over-eaten himself after being exhausted by a long Popish fast," brought a stroke of apoplexy upon Lord Eaglescairn; and, that branch of his family thus becoming extinct, he was succeeded in the title by a very distant cousin, who, "not being able to carry the Church [of England] his own way, quarrelled with it altogether, suddenly associated himself with the Jesuits, and retired to one of their institutions near Bath." We shall come to him again when we speak of converts, for, like Sir Evan M'Alpine, we desire to make a "proper distinction between families in which the Romanism was hereditary, and those in whom, like Lord Eaglescairn, it had recently arisen, from vanity, love of power, and love of excitement"—these, as all the world knows, being potent factors in conversions. But we must not forget the "ignorant villagers" who

were summoned [to the chapel] several times a day, to hear Latin prayers inaudibly muttered, and where they learnt only the bodily exercise which profiteth nothing, to wear scapulars round their necks, to kneel before a wooden image of St. Benedict [one would have suspected the Jesuits of a preference for St. Ignatius], and to count their beads, amidst a perfect toyshop of trifles and trinkets,[1] relics and rosaries.

[1] These must have been the "trinkets of Rome," which Dr. Benson once accused some of his clergy of "fingering."

The Laity.

No rational education, nor intellectual piety, accompanied the injunctions laid on these poor deluded peasants to buy expensive indulgences and perform laborious penances, both of which combined to keep them in hopeless degradation of mind, as well as in most thoroughly pillaged poverty.[1]

One more picture must be given of "the Popish half of Clanmarina," which presented "one scene of universal filth, ignorance, profligacy, discontent, and ferocity, only to be matched in priest-ridden Ireland." Father Eustace had promised miraculously to cure the potato blight, and assembled all his ragged votaries round the Holy Well of St. Bridget, where the priest now stood surrounded by a crowd of votaries calling on their patron saint to remedy this disease. Many wore charms and scapulars blessed by Father Eustace to keep them from harm, and they all carried beads, candles, crucifixes, ashes, oil, images and pictures. In a recess near the entrance to the chapel, several squalid-looking villagers were kneeling before an image of St. Bridget, and frantically muttering Latin prayers which they could not understand.[2]

We must leave the villagers to the delights indicated above—which must have afforded a pleasant relief after their more usual exercise of "crawling round inside the chapel of St. Bridget on their bare knees, stopping at times before the altars of various saints to offer them prayers"—as it is desirable to know something of how Catholics in higher walks of life conduct themselves.

The laughing hours at Eaglescairn were spent by the juvenile members of the party in a state of strenuous idleness, for it is thought better by Papists for the young to do anything rather than to think. Mr. Ambrose [it must be remembered that he was a Jesuit] having incidentally mentioned that the monks of St. Bernard amuse themselves during the long winter evening in whist, round games

[1] *Beatrice*, chap. ii.   [2] *Ibid.*, chap. xxii.

and dancing, Lord Iona said he thought it too good an example not to be followed. He joyously ordered the Highland piper immediately, and a gay scene took place.

Among the guests was Lady Anne Darlington. Like so many of the characters in *Beatrice*, she ultimately became a Protestant, and married Sir Allan (of whom we have heard in a previous chapter); but when we first make her acquaintance she intends to become a nun. "Father Eustace paints a perfect castle-in-the-air life in a convent, where she is to be a good fairy, performing miracles, manufacturing sweetmeats, sweeping her own cell, making her own bed, and seeing supernatural visions;"[1] and this picture was attractive to one who "lived in an incessant April shower of imaginary distresses." Lady Anne "was the very idol of society," and no wonder; for although she dressed with "almost conventual simplicity," and "looked to Beatrice like a beautiful corpse, or the ghost that might haunt an old abbey of some murdered nun," "there was in all [her] movements a singular grace; her manner was natural as the wild-bird in a hedge; her laugh was soft and musical; her, clear, ringing, lark-like voice had an enchantment in every tone," and her singing "wrapped every sense in ecstasy." Lady Anne kept in her boudoir a "large collection of painted missals and prints," and "a sort of extempore altar," furnished with an image of St. Veronica, a *prie dieu*, two candles and a crucifix.

"You see," said Lady Anne gravely, "to a person like me, only in the middle classes of intellect, what an advantage it is to have no exercise of mind required. I go over my rosary twice a day, and am not required to understand a syllable of it. The rest of my devotional time is filled up with incessantly repeated *Ave Marias*."

[1] *Beatrice*, chap. xxii.

She was kept in stern subjection by Father Eustace, who often made her "do penance for having felt a craving to eat buttered toast or even a bit of dry bread," which provoked Beatrice to reminiscences of "that poor young Oxonian, Froude, who killed himself in useless austerities for imaginary guilt." Lady Anne took Beatrice to a convent, where they were just in time to see "one of the nuns anathematised for eating food when she was ordered to fast, having been detected in the act of devouring raw vegetables, like any hungry animal, in the garden." I cannot resist the temptation to quote the description of this function :—

On the floor of the chapel a black cloth had been carefully spread, adorned in the centre with a white cross, and the smell of medicated incense was almost intoxicating. When Lady Anne stole in, followed by Beatrice, the candles on the altar were at that very moment extinguished by Father Eustace, who was pronouncing in a sepulchral tone before a glittering crucifix, as if his tongue were almost frozen with horror, a long, gloomy, and most awful anathema on the trembling culprit, a young nun of most emaciated aspect, after which he raised on high for a moment the lighted torch he held in his hand which he dashed on the ground so that the flame became extinguished. It was a scene most exciting to the senses, the passions and the imaginations of unaccustomed persons, but the nuns began immediately counting their beads, and looking carelessly around them.

The way in which religion is made attractive to young Catholics is depicted by Lord Iona, who, on hearing that Sir Allan M'Alpine was fasting for a whole week, and therefore could not be allowed to take a glass of wine, whispered to Beatrice :—

"Well do I guess the sort of thing M'Alpine goes through, from my own experience. I nearly sunk under it myself; but Father Eustace, then my confessor, was proud of my 'frost-bit feet and dirty serge,' crusts of bread for a fortnight, and midnight vigils. As a boy I used to pick up the crumbs thrown out to the sparrows, and often slept standing or walking. M'Alpine is hardly ever now quite awake, for sleep steals over him against his will, or without his knowledge, but one cannot trick him into unconsciously eating."

I reluctantly omit any account of the "recluse"—who lived in a cell containing a wooden bench to sleep on, a rustic table, "something that seemed intended for bread, though black and hard as a piece of coal," an earthen jar of water, "purposely rendered nauseous by a mixture of bitter herbs," a gaudily decorated missal, a crucifix of stucco, a rosary of amber beads, and a large image of St. Bridget dressed in blue satin and gold [1]—because space must be found for a picture of a Catholic death-bed.

Lord Eaglescairn lay dying "in a lofty and spacious room hung with tapestry and pictures, and on a bed hung with curtains of the richest velvet. . . . Father Eustace sat beside him alone, sprinkling his face occasionally with holy water from St. Victore's well, and holding up a blessed chaplet in *articulo mortis.*" These consolations, however, failed to comfort the dying peer; "he had received the last offices of the Church—no mourning relatives were permitted to approach the expiring sufferer—nothing was left for him to do but to die," and for this he seemed unwilling. The fact of it was that he had defrauded Beatrice of her inheritance in the interests

[1] The recluse also possessed "a collection of relics, rosaries, medals and images: she had also a multitudinous picture-gallery, portraits of various saints, many of which were believed, on the authority of Father Eustace, to nod, wink and bleed, when for special occasions required to exhibit their powers."

of the Church at the instigation of Father Eustace, who, "like the Duke of Burgundy's confessor," had promised to take upon himself the punishment due to the crime—just as Anglican parsons are reported to offer to be responsible for certain of their penitents whom they induce to remain in the Church of England. Father Eustace, "in a low tone of fierce determination, his whole form expanding with rage," endeavoured to prevent Lord Eaglescairn from telling his son: "It is my affair," said he, "that you do not injure the Church by an unseemly death," and he forced the dying man to receive from his hand a sleeping-draught. But his lordship "by a sudden gesture directed the eye of Father Eustace for an instant towards the door, and during that moment secretly poured the whole potion noiselessly on the bedclothes," which must have made them very uncomfortable. Lord Eaglescairn then feigned sleep, and Father Eustace, "summoning the old sick nurse, who was studying the *Visions of St. Anthony*," left the room. No sooner were nurse and patient left together, than the former was despatched to Lord Iona, whom she aroused by "scratching upon the curtains in Jesuit fashion." He at once obeyed the summons, and his father made a clean breast of it. "Bury my faults in oblivion," he said, at the end of his confession, "though that is a funeral much too honourable for such crimes." Then "a heavy hurried step was heard lumbering along the passage"—for in the excitement of the moment Father Eustace had forgotten to glide—and the earl died before the priest could enter the room.

Ireland is naturally the scene of countless volumes of Protestant fiction, not including the reports of the various societies which have for many years spent much money to little purpose in endeavouring to convince the Irish people of the advantages of Protestantism. Here are one or two brief extracts from *The Manuscript Man, or, The Bible in Ireland,* by Miss E. H. Walshe.[1]

The Irish year is almost as full of holidays as the Italian one; and from the same cause—the arrangements of the Roman Church. To work during any of these tabooed portions of time is a venial sin, only expiated by penance imposed after confession. No matter how favourable the weather for seed-time or reaping (in a climate proverbially fickle), the peasant dares not use spade or sickle on Lady Day in spring or Lady Day in harvest, or a score other equally sacred seasons; whereas, if the Sabbath happens to suit for saving hay or stacking oats or pitting potatoes, he takes God's day without a thought of wrong.

In Ireland the priest says Mass in "alb and cope,"[2] and

the peasantry really believe that these sacerdotal garments make the wearers holy, sinless for the time being; nay, that whoever dies in the dress, passes into paradise.

The women wind up the evening with the

usual rosary on the beads. This meant the Creed repeated on the pendant cross, thirteen Hail Marys and three Paternosters on sixteen beads, and a fourth Paternoster on a large ball which they call "the dixeth."[3]

Of its meaning they know little: Kate O'Toole, the heroine of *The Light of the Gospel,* a penny story already referred to,

night after night retired to murmur over her litanies, and tell her beads, introducing arithmetic into religion with a

---

[1] Religious Tract Society, 1889. Price 3d.
[2] *L.c.,* 103, 107.   [3] *L.c.,* 109.

wholesome ignorance of what worship is, and how far removed from any arithmetical measure of acceptability; [while] her inquiring father opened his Testament at the mark which indicated the spot where he had left off the night before, and read on for an hour of two by the firelight. . . . While his only son [an ecclesiastical student] was being crammed with the learning of Gregory, the sophistry of Liguori, the decrees of Trent, the father, over his turf and log fire, was being gently taught by a silent but eloquent teacher, how false and how ruinous all human guides are to the soul which seeks God.

Poor Paddy's Cabin,[1] a tale of the potato famine, which had a large circulation and has often been reprinted, is "a true picture of the real state of things in Ireland," and a warning against "the portentous influence which is creeping like an incubus over the bosom of our once free constitution." Paddy, a convert from Popery, was an efficient 'expounder of the Bible: "You see," said he, "there are people who are able to kill the soul—that is, as I thinks, when they can frighten 'em, as the priest does, from God's Word;" and he "very ingeniously changed" the prayers he had learnt as a boy, by substituting our Lord's name for our Lady's—with somewhat startling results one would think; it is not easy to imagine the "Hail, Mary," or "Hail, Holy Queen," thus altered. He had also studied English history, and was as convinced as Mr. Collette that Henry VIII. "lived and died a lump of a Roman. All the Protestants had to do with him was this—he quarrelled with the Pope, and as they say, 'When rogues fall out, honest men came by their own,' Henry, out of spite to the Pope, wouldn't let him put the people down, as he used to

[1] *Poor Paddy's Cabin, or, Slavery in Ireland.* By an Irishman. Wertheim & Macintosh. Third edition, 1854.

do before; and the honest men came by their own." No simpler account of the Reformation could be penned.

It appears from the story that one motive for the emigration which occurred at this period was "*an instinctive feeling that they were slaves of the priest*,"[1] who "led them to think the present landed proprietors of Ireland were strangers and robbers who had no real right in the soil." Father Mathew's movement, we learn, "not only failed of any important good, but actually tended to foster and increase the influence of priestcraft and superstition. It is truly a humiliating sight to see a number of human beings kneeling in the mud to receive the blessing of a poor fellow-sinner as if he were invested with deity, as those creatures do to the priest who administers the pledge."[2]

The Irish abroad as at home—with the exception of those who embrace Protestantism—display ignorance and superstition, tinged with fanaticism, in almost equal proportion. There are some delightful stage Irishmen in *The Six Sisters of the Valleys*,[3] who were driven from their country by Cromwell, and took service in the Piedmontese army. Here is a specimen of their conversation :—

"By St. Pathrick's thumbscrews," said one to his companion, as they approached the entrance of the valley of

[1] Italics in original.

[2] It will probably be news to most of my readers that the temperance movement was regarded as a Jesuit plot: but this view is set forth at length in a book of 300 pages, entitled "*Protestant Jesuitism*, by a Protestant," published in New York in 1836. The author says: "Having viewed the Temperance measures as occupying a leading position in that system of Jesuitism which has been set up in this country, and as it has, at last, come to so clear a development of such a design, it seemed to him pertinent, and somewhat important, to make thorough work in exposing it."

[3] See p. 67.

Lucerna, "what's this Goshen we're promished here to make up for Ould Ireland? Shure, then, we must be ready to labour in the extermination of heretics."

"The land looks well, Misther Donoghue; those high mountains are bigger than our Magillicuddys Reeks; but I fear we shall not get as good a dhrap of ould *potheen* here."

"By Saint Pathrick's shillelah," said the second speaker, "here's a roomy shebeen shop. Halloa, Fathers, *Patres conscripti*, as my young masther used to say," cried he, addressing the monks; "faith, I want to see if there's a jewel of a girl here can darn my rags, for the snow sthrikes could right through."

Here is another example :—

"Marcy on us, here's a blaze," cried O'Donoghue [they had just set fire to a Waldensian chapel]. "The clargy want to warm their feet, and it's right on the 1st of January when the frost is nipping our toes. I'll bet his riverince would like to clap that Sassenach on the top, and I should like to be afther roastin' some pratees. But I must lind a hand. God an' the blissed Mother and the thrue Church for iver."

O'Donoghue also swore "by the jawbone of Pathrick, the serpent-killer," and "by the middle knuckle of St. Francis." His French companions apostrophized "the rags of Peter the Hermit," and addressed heretics thus :—

"Come, be quick," shouted Villalmin Roche, "or we'll throw you into the courtyard for an airing, and then pour you out some hot toast and water. If not, Father Malvicino will speak to his confessor with horns, and he'll give you some hot toast without the water."

It will be observed that both Irishmen and Frenchmen indulge in the same method of invocation which characterized the Italian Abbot Malvicino; this picturesque practice seems to have been general among Catholics in the seventeenth century.

It must not be supposed from the dates of publication of some of these volumes that Protestant fiction is a thing of the past, or that the demand for it has slackened. The Religious Tract Society—one of the largest publishers of Protestant "religious" literature—is at the present time (December, 1898) advertising payments of £50, £35 and £21 for "three stories on the Present-day Aspects of the Controversy with Rome," and I have some thoughts of entering into competition for one of them. Moreover, the same highly respectable society says that "the question of the hour" is, "Is England drifting Romewards?" and recommends "all interested in the question" to read various works, including certain stories, one of which I now propose to consider.

The Lord of that Land, or, Margherita Brandini's Deliverance, by Margaret S. Comrie, lets in a flood of light on the ways of lay-folk in Italy. It would appear that, left to themselves, they are well-intentioned and even exemplary people; but "the eternal note of sadness" comes in—need I say that it is sounded by the Jesuits? But to the story.

Margherita Brandini was sixteen years old when the story opens, and was occupied in throwing *soldi* into a pool and invoking a water-witch. But the witch did not respond, so Margherita said, somewhat irrelevantly: "O Holy Mother, thou goest in search of the miserable, pray to Jesus for me! Sweet Heart of Mary, send me happiness!" Then she thought aloud of Aunt Cecilia, who led "the life of a saint, with her fastings and penances," but who was not cheerful, and of two cousins who were heretics, and always happy. Then she thought of "what was coming, what every day brings nearer," and moaned and sobbed.

The Laity.

It is not difficult to guess "what was coming." " Years ago she made a vow to enter a convent," and Aunt Cecilia and Father Gasparo told her that, if she didn't keep it, she would " bring a terrible curse " upon herself. They also showed her a picture of purgatory, with the face of her mother in it, and made it clear to her that the only way of releasing the late Signora Brandini "from the flames" was by entering the convent. It was a hard case, for Colonel Brandini "had no money to pay for Masses," the tariff in Italy being apparently high; and Margherita was assured that it was necessary she should take the vows, and "dedicate her whole fortune to the Church for the sake of her mother's soul." And she didn't want to do it.

Madame Corvietti—otherwise Aunt Cecilia—and Father Gasparo had several points in common. They were both "tall black figures," they listened at doors, and glided about "with slow noiseless steps," and were as unscrupulous " as they make 'em "—to adopt the expression of a young friend of mine who is regrettably addicted to slang. No one could have doubted, directly he appeared on the scene, that Father Gasparo was a Jesuit—he had all the marks—although it is not till page 301 that we are assured of the fact.

There was a time, in the days before he became a theological student, when Alphonso Gasparo would have scorned as utterly false and mean the underhand dealings which without scruple he now employed to further what he called the interests of Holy Mother Church. By nature young Gasparo had been endowed with noble instincts and lofty aims; but a long course of training in the Jesuit College in Rome had, as a matter of course, succeeded in blunting and confusing his moral perceptions.[1]

[1] P. 301.

Gasparo was playing his last card, for Margherita had been too much for "the father confessor" and her aunt together; but he had not completed his second sentence when Count Brandini, whose sentiments he was atrociously misrepresenting, looked in at the window, and the Jesuit, "with the cowardice of a guilty conscience, which had no thought beyond that of his own safety, made with undignified haste for the door. Like a candle snuffed out by finger and thumb, Father Alphonso Gasparo went out." "True to the last to his false creed," however, "he tenaciously held his sole remaining card." This was a bogus letter, which had been "tampered with," and with which Father Gasparo tried to impose upon Count Brandini; but in vain. Jesuit as he was, he was taken in hand by the count's kinsman, Cardinal Borelli, who was going to find him "a post across the seas, in some country where the climate will be less stimulating to his ecclesiastical zeal."

The Jesuit's tool, Madame Corvietti, was detected by Colonel Maxwell Brandini—he had added his *fiancée's* name to his own before his marriage was sanctioned by her guardians—in the plot to force Margherita into the convent, so the colonel sent her away. She went to the Convent of the Sacred Heart in Rome, "where, in the peace of a blessed consecration," she hoped to pass the remainder of her life. But the colonel, anxious to dispel any illusion she might have cherished—though he could hardly have been speaking from personal knowledge—pointed out to her that "the lot of a nun at the best means life-long captivity, a hopeless, dreary existence spent in a round of hard servitude, profitless often to God and man." The poor lady would have been well enough had it not been for Father Gasparo, and even tried to escape from the course of deceit and fraud upon which she had entered; yet when your father confessor tells you that " though your appointed service may appear to you hard, even crooked, but, in the fulfilment of your vow of unquestioning obedience to Holy Mother Church, all acts of piety prescribed by your directors become not only justifiable but meritorious "—what are you to do?

Colonel Brandini, although he turned up trumps in the end, was undoubtedly a bad lot. " I joined the Church of Rome not from religious conviction, but merely from self-interest. My religious profession, therefore," he continued, " was but a hollow sham. I did evil that good may come—the doctrine of the Church that I now call mine." This is all very well, but it seems rather hard to make the Church responsible for his motives before he joined it. Then he dealt with the Jesuit and his accomplice : " In the name of religion your aunt and Father Gasparo have plotted to secure you and your fortune to the Church. In their eyes the end was holy, and therefore the means, however false, were justified."

It need not be said that Margherita did not " pray to God, but only to the Virgin Mary " : and of course the worthy old priest—who seems to have been a Protestant in disguise—though he had a copy of the Holy Scriptures somewhere, had never read it. He read the " appointed daily portions " in the Breviary, however, which was something, and Margherita's Protestant cousins came and sang him Protestant hymns, which pleased the good old man. Purgatory is defined as the place " where the good are condemned to be burnt in the fire till they are purified from their sins unabsolved on earth." Margherita, although ignorant of the Bible, was well acquainted with the lives of the saints :—

There was St. Christina, for instance; in order to release souls from purgatory by her own good works, she came back from heaven to earth again, and walked into burning ovens, and kept under the ice of the river for six days and more at a time, and more than once she was whirled round and round the wheel of a water-mill.

Perhaps the most striking feature of the book is the account of Subiaco. Bruce (one of the Protestant cousins) "sees something white glancing in and out among the green"; it was "a procession of the brothers," who were allowed once a week to take a walk outside the monastery grounds.

In wondering amazement Ailsa gazed at the white-robed figures, for the most part gaunt and haggard, with heavy, listless steps. Who were they, that pitiable band? They were men, but men, alas! in whom all manly instincts, all liberty of spirit, all noble aspirations of the free-born soul, had died long since. The casket was there, but the jewel it contained had by an iron foot been trampled on and crushed.

These extracts will show sufficiently the class of story which is recommended to "all interested in the question—Is England drifting Romewards?" How it bears upon the question, I do not know; but I think all would agree with Ailsa in gazing upon the "white-robed" Benedictines "with wondering amazement."

One word, however, must be said as to the Protestants in the story and their conduct. Bruce, aged twelve—one of the two Scotch cousins—comments thus upon the vow of silence taken by the white-robed Benedictines: "If only I could cut out the Pope's tongue, and lend it out by the hour to those poor fellows in turn: I shouldn't wear out my own tongue afterwards in reminding them to send back old Leo's to him." When he hears his cousin say the rosary, he says: "If you believe God listens to such gabble-gabbling, surely you must think He has very little to do." St. Peter's is to Bruce the place "where the Pope's toe and the Pope live." "If the quickest way to grow into a saint is to try to half kill oneself, why doesn't the Pope, with all the priests and cardinals, open the Inquisition and shut themselves in there, and then try all the tortures upon themselves, one after the other?" is another of his sapient remarks.

Ailsa is a little prig, and her arguments are of the usual Protestant stamp. When Margherita says she is going into a convent, Ailsa says, "There is nothing at all in the Bible about convents"—an argument which might be employed with equal force against the steam-engine and the printing-press—"even Mary, the Mother of Jesus, didn't go into a convent when Jesus died." It is impossible to believe that even Protestant children talk such nonsense as this.

The author herself takes no pains to conceal her own sentiments. The statue of St. Peter she describes as "the so-called apostle, an imbecile-looking black image on a chair of state near the high altar"—which of course it is not: of the clergy she says: "With their soiled linen, greasy black robes, slouching gait, and air of sensual indolence, the members of the Roman priesthood are singularly unprepossessing". When the old priest is asked what the Popes did, "there rises up before him with startling vividness a vision of the fiends in human form whose lives of vice and cruelty had been the execration of the world and the scandal of the Church, that very Church whose voice and authority nevertheless had commanded mankind to reverence these monsters as the Vicars of Jesus Christ."[1]

The above summary and extracts give some idea of the kind of story recommended and issued by the Religious Tract Society—a body, be it remembered, which enjoys the patronage and support of a large number of the leading ecclesiastics and lay members of the Church of England.

I found a good deal of information as to the habits of Italian Catholics in a work entitled *Sketches and Stories of Life in Italy*, by an Italian countess— also published by the Religious Tract Society— which I picked up at a pleasant little hotel at Weesen, on the Wollenzee: it had been "presented by the Colonial and Continental Church Society for the use of visitors"—I quote from the printed label inside the cover. The Italian countess tells us in her preface that her anxiety is that Italians should learn "the great truth—the rejection of which is the centre of Papal error—that Christ and *not* the Virgin is the one Mediator between God and man." The antithesis which is commonly assumed to occur between poverty and honesty—"he was born of poor but honest parents" —evidently exists between Catholicism and morality: "*Although* she had been bred in Roman Catholicism, Maddelena was a girl of high and dignified morality" (p. 124). The people of the book were very ignorant: "the dwellers in these abodes were all more or less in the habit of going to Mass"—*O si sic omnia!*—"but knowing no more of vital religion than the little figures of saints to which they prayed," apparently at Mass (p. 69). Their ignorance extended to their own language: "A strict Roman Catholic flogged himself

[1] P. 215.

during Quaresima before an image of the Madonna crying '*Miserare mia!*'" (p. 103). This was an odd remark; but it is yet more surprising to read that "the monks began to chant the *Miserere*—De profundis clamavi ad Te Domine." The unreasonableness with which fathers insist (p. 209) upon their paternal rights is exemplified by an unseemly struggle over a baby which "the priest tried to steal away and baptise into the Roman Church, the [Catholic] father assisting him; his Christian wife Emma set her face against it, declaring that her child should be taught to 'venerate her Creator in the days of her youth' and not be subject to the errors and crafts of Roman priests."

Among the numerous volumes issued in cheap cloth binding at incredibly low prices, and largely sold at drapers' shops as well as by small booksellers, are some by Augusta J. Evans Wilson. One of these, *Inez, a Tale of the Alamos*, claims a high place in Protestant fiction. It must be remembered, and I must be excused for again recurring to the fact, that books of this kind circulate by the hundred thousand; and it cannot be doubted that the ignorant Protestant bases his ideas of Popery largely upon the material thus put before him: did not a cousin of my own tell me that all she knew about Catholics she had learned from *Beatrice*?

The scene of this story is laid in Mexico, and shortly after the opening of the story, "the vesper bells chimed out on the evening air."

Even as the Moslem kneels at sunset towards the "Holy City," so punctiliously does the devout Papist bend for vesper prayers.

It will be seen, however, that the bending does not take place in church, unless the population of the parish was limited to twelve. So few of us have been to Mexico that the following description of the internal arrangements and ceremonies prevalent in Mexican churches cannot fail to be of interest :—

Over the division of the long room hung a silken curtain, concealing three niches, which contained an image of the "Virgin," the "Child," and, in the centre one, a tall gilt cross. Heavy silver candlesticks were placed in front of each niche, and a dozen candles were now burning dimly. A variety of relics, too numerous to mention, were scattered on the altar, and, in addition, several silver goblets, and a massive bowl for holding "holy water." About a dozen devotees were present; all kneeling on the damp, hard floor. The silk curtain which concealed the altar was drawn aside, with due solemnity, by two boys habited in red flannel petticoats, over which hung a loose white slip. The officiating priest was seen kneeling before the altar, with his lips pressed to the foot of the cross. He retained his position for several moments, then rising, conducted the ceremonies in a calm, imposing manner. When these were concluded, and all had departed save the two boys, who still knelt before the Virgin, he beckoned them to him, and speaking a few words in Spanish, ended by pointing to the door and uttering, emphatically, "Go." Crossing themselves as they passed the images, they disappeared through a side door, and the priest was left alone.

The countenance of the priest, Father Mazzolin, "was that of one well versed in intrigue"; "a large amount of Jesuit determination was expressed in his iris, blended with cunning, malignity and fierceness." When a Mexican came to see him and forgot "the reverence due to the marble images," he "pointed to them with a stern glance, crossing himself as he did so"; and Juan at once took the hint, "went down on his knees, said an Ave Maria and laid a Mexican dollar on the altar," thinking himself lucky to get off so cheaply. Far differently did Inez fare when she went to confession and accused herself of missing "Mass, vespers, and many holy ordinances of our most holy Church." For these and other peccadilloes, Father Mazzolin imposed the following penance—one wonders what he would have done in a really serious case :—

"I enjoin upon you, as penance for the omission of the holy ordinances of our most holy Church, five Credos when you hear the matin bell, twelve Paters when noon comes round, and five Aves at vespers. These shall you repeat, kneeling upon the hard floor, with the crucifix before you, and your rosary in your hand. In addition, you must repair to a cell of San Jose, and there remain one month. Moreover, you shall see and speak to none, save the holy sisters. And now, my daughter, I would absolve you."

I am sorry I did not know of Father Mazzolin when I was writing about priests, for he would have proved a valuable addition to my clerical portrait gallery. As it is, I must confine myself to his flock. There was Mr. Hamilton, for example, who although not a Papist when in health, succumbed to the Father's influence on his deathbed, especially when the latter "muttered an oath between his teeth and spoke in an unknown tongue." This is how Mr. Hamilton died :—

The sufferer had been placed for convenience on a low couch, and was supported by pillows in an upright position. A dozen candles burnt around him, and a cloud of incense wreathed slowly along the wall. The room had been profusely sprinkled with holy water, and a chalice, containing the consecrated wafer, stood near. Father Mazzolin, attired in a surplice, ornamented with the insignia of his order, stood beside the bed, holding in one hand a superbly bound volume—in the other, a silver cup containing oil.

After a moment's pause he opened the book, and hurriedly read in a low, muttering tone, a Latin service of several pages. At the conclusion he carefully poured out a few drops of the oil, and just touched the palms of the sufferer's hands, and the soles of his feet, bidding him at the same time cross himself. Perceiving that he was utterly unable to do so, he hastily signed the figure, and resumed his reading. How long he would have gabbled on it is impossible to say, but a gasping sound from the dying man declared that dissolution was at hand, and, snatching the chalice, he hastily administered the wafer, which was swallowed with difficulty.

Florence Hamilton became a Catholic—and Inez, who had "listened to her aves and paters," told Mary Irving about it. Now Mary was a staunch Protestant, and promptly took Florry to task. Having conclusively shown that the teaching of the Fathers was erroneous, Mary (whose knowledge seems to have been "extensive and peculiar") proceeded to consult them. She pursued Florry with unrelenting ardour through several pages, summing up her arguments by saying :—

"You should remember that the promulgation of Papal doctrines, and the aggrandisement of the Romish Church, is the only aim of its priesthood; consequently, all means which conduce to this great object are unscrupulously employed. Even crime is sanctioned where the good of the Church can be promoted."

This made Florence unhappy; and her Aunt Lizzy, a devout Papist, went and told Father Mazzolin about it. But she need not have done this, for Florence herself went and confronted him with Bible quotations, whereupon he said :—

"I swear, if you do not hear and abide by what I say, your father's soul will remain for ever in purgatory, where it justly belongs."

Fortunately Mary, "who had approached unobserved," overheard this remark, and there was a royal row, in the course of which Father Mazzolin informed Florence that he was her brother. Mr. Hamilton had had "a past," and his son swore that his " soul should linger in damnation " if his behests were not fulfilled. The Jesuit seems to have been imperfectly instructed, but the painful surgical operation which he had undergone would account for a good deal :—

"Know you not, girl," he said, "that when a Jesuit priest takes the oath of his order, he tears his heart from his breast and lays it at the feet of his superior? Appeal not to ties of relationship: we repudiate them, and pity is unknown among us."

Mary then gave Florence a lecture on purgatory and indulgences, and contrasted Catholic with Protestant countries in the manner of Dr. Horton, whom she seems to have anticipated. She went on for pages and pages, and it is no wonder that Florence succumbed; besides, if she had not, where would be the moral of the story? Inez, too, "died without the pale of the Church," having throughout the book been more than a match for the machinations of Father Mazzolin, whose capabilities, as usual, seem to have been much overrated. There was an awful scene at the deathbed, and the language used on both sides was dreadful.

The story contains somewhere in the background plottings and a war, but they do not seem to matter. Inez was a good deal mixed up in the business and, had it not been for her, numerous unpleasant things would have happened. Even as it was there was something like a massacre, owing to the treachery of the Mexicans ;

> But what they fought each other for
> I could not well make out.

I must now say a few words about converts—those, I mean, who do not, like most of those in Protestant fiction, revert to Protestantism. Cardinal Newman's masterly summary of the various explanations given by non-Catholics to account for conversions is familiar to every one.[1] Dr. Littledale, if my memory serves me, has a low opinion of converts, and speaks of their moral deterioration; but it must be remembered that they are, according to Protestant authorities, often secured by very doubtful stratagems, and by inducements which clearly have an undue influence on their minds. I remember that at a Protestant school where I was once a pupil, the denunciation of those who "compass sea and land to make one proselyte," was always applied to Catholic priests, and the result was said to be similar to that which occurred in the case of the Scribes and Pharisees.

Their eagerness is easily explained: "Father Eustace asserts that for every Protestant brought round to Romanism, the successful Papist is saved an hundred years of purgatory; therefore now, upon a principle of the merest selfishness, it becomes of tremendous importance to carry over one individual." So said Lady Edith,[2] and it was therefore only natural that "Lord Eaglescairn and his whole family" should have "become frantically eager about making converts." Bessie M'Ronald was a victim of their zeal: and by what arts did they accomplish their fell purpose! When her lover denounced to Lady Edith what had been done—while Bessie, "with her trembling hands clasped together, and the countenance

[1] *Lectures on the Present Position of Catholics in England*, vi.
[2] *Beatrice*, ch. xxi.

The Laity.

of a corpse, sat immovably cowering in a chair "—he

hurled upon the table, while his pale compressed lips quivered with angry contempt, a rosary of amber beads, a relic of decayed bone in a small glass case, which broke as it fell, an image of St. Bridget in stucco, and an old tooth, fit only for a charnel-house, some ancient iron instruments of torture, a lock of odd-looking red hair, said to be St. Bridget's, and a missal richly decorated with brass corners and clasps.

"Such are the attractions which Rome holds out to those whom she seeks to enrol among her deluded votaries," as Lady Edith might have observed ; for Bessie had not yet become a Catholic, although when she said she could not "attend regularly at a Popish chapel, Lady Eaglescairn looked aghast with indignation, and said imperatively, 'Pshaw, nonsense!'" This remark, coupled with the small museum mentioned above, effected Bessie's conversion, whereupon she used "the discipline twice every day, and requested that her bed might be stuffed with knotty lumps of wood, and broken pieces of pottery." She also complied with the rule of Eaglescairn Castle, where all wore "coarse hair-shirts from the neck to the knees, like that of the exemplary saint, Sancia Cariglio"; and beneath it wore "a large iron cross, spiked with nails."

Such violent delights as these, however, would not have been appreciated by Lord Deloraine, whom the histrionic attractions of Rome allured to her embraces. (One remarkable feature of Protestant fiction, I may be allowed to say parenthetically, is the hypnotic influence which it possesses. I am continually struggling, and not always successfully, against the spell exercised by Miss Sinclair's style.)

His little atom of intellect found gratification occasionally in the stately ceremonials and exciting music of the Popish Church. Here [his] languid senses were lulled into a state of dreamy unconsciousness, while he sat as if at a morning concert, or a sort of Sunday opera, feeling himself exceedingly good and pious, in partaking for some hours [!] of melodious sounds and intoxicating perfumes, as well as in watching the bowing and pirouetting and processions of the magnificently dressed priests.[1]

"Another way"—to quote the cookery-books—of attracting the unwary is that narrated by Miss Tonna—who wrote much under the name of "Charlotte Elizabeth"—in a book bearing the deceptive title *Chapters on Flowers*, which has more than once been catalogued under the general heading "Botany." Miss Tonna was indeed *mulier fortis;* we have it on the authority of Miss A. J. E. Wilson, in the work from which I have quoted above.

The Pope of imperial Rome, surrounded as he is with luxury, magnificence, and hosts of scarlet-liveried cardinals, who stand in readiness to convey his mandates to the remotest corners of the earth, has been made to tremble on his throne by the pen of a feeble woman. The truthful delineations of Charlotte Elizabeth started his Holiness of the Vatican, and the assistant conclave of learned cardinals trembled lest their laity of the Green Isle should catch a glimpse of light. A bull was quickly fulminated against her heretical productions. Alas! when, when will the Romish Church burst the iron bands which begirt her?[2]

One would have thought that the Romish Church would have been more likely to strengthen than to burst the bands which begirt so stout a Protestant champion; but the pronoun in the last sentence probably refers to the Church rather than to Miss

---

[1] *London Homes*, p. 16.   [2] *Inez*, chap. xviii.

Tonna. What was "the monk that shook the world" in comparison with this noble woman? There is a Protestant hymn which tells how

> Satan trembles when he sees
> The weakest saint upon his knees:

but even this hardly presents so striking a picture as that of "the Pope of imperial Rome" shivering on his throne before Charlotte Elizabeth. Cannot Mrs. Arbuthnot obtain for publication in *The Protestant Woman* a translation of the bull which was fulminated against Miss Tonna's books? It would be a standing testimony of the futility of Rome's attempts to fetter the Protestant press.

To resume. Miss Tonna tells us in *Chapters on Flowers* that there had been a big haul of a Protestant widow and all her daughters, under the following circumstances. The husband of the widow (and father of the daughters) having been a Catholic, "a number of priests," in accordance with Catholic custom,

assembled to perform offices for the departed soul, during the time that the corpse lay in the house, and so well did they improve their opportunity, that the widow and all her daughters renounced Protestantism after the funeral, with the exception of E——.

To overcome her conscientious repugnance, the most nefarious means were resorted to; a pretended miracle performed by some relic, failed to convert, though it staggered her; and they then had recourse to one of the foul stratagems, so common in gaining proselytes from among the young and imaginative. They contrived that, in the dead of night, a figure resembling her deceased father, of whom she was very fond, should appear to her, stating that he had obtained permission to revisit the earth, for the sacred purpose of solemnly assuring her that the faith in which he died was the only passport to heaven. This succeeded—she never recovered from the shock; but she renounced her religion, and took the veil.

Charlotte Elizabeth did her best for E——, whom she knew personally, but apparently in vain. Still there was hope, for "many a recantation openly made, is nowhere registered but in heaven, and in the dark bosoms of those who suppress the tale." Charlotte, moreover, had her own faith to look to, for the nuns, she says, "had engaged the help of a seminary of Jesuits, not far off, to proselytise ME"—seemingly by sending her "one of the most specious and dangerous works ever penned, Milner's *End of Controversy*," also described as an "artful web of deep and diabolical sophistry." Fortunately she had an antidote in the pages of "the beloved," if untrustworthy, "martyrologist, that paragon of memorialists, John Fox," of whose work she, in later years, issued an abridged edition. "I loved John Fox dearly, even before I could well support one of his ponderous volumes; and many a time my little heart has throbbed almost to bursting, when, having deposited the book on a chair, and opened its venerable leaves, I leant upon the page." It was certainly unwise in one so young to lift so heavy a weight.

Miss Emma Jane Worboise, a dull and voluminous writer, beloved in Evangelical circles, devoted one of her novels to "the story of a pervert"; we learn from the *Athenæum* of 26th February, 1898, that this was one of the most popular of her books, and it was the first of a reissue of her contributions to literature. "*I have not been writing fiction*," she says (in italics) at the end of *Overdale: A Tale for the Times;* "the same story is being told daily in every county of England."

The Laity.

This terrible monotony (for it is a very dull story) will continue "so long as the errors of ritualism, the great heresy and schism of the nineteenth century, prevail among us"; so it looks as if it would continue for some time.

Overdale is the name of a village, not of a person, the spiritual oversight of which was committed to a High Church parson named Aylmer. He was a widower when he married Agatha; but he "sinned in forming the marriage tie [twice] against his conscience," and ultimately deserted her, in obedience to the dictates of Vallance, who was a Jesuit in the disguise of a clergyman. Mr. and Mrs. Aylmer had a painful scene. She said she was his wife, and implored Eustace not to look through "the hoodwinked spectacles of that crafty man Vallance." But Mr. Aylmer had gone too far to retract. He said, "I must in due course profess myself a Catholic"; and when Agatha rejoined, "But you need not continue to be a clergyman," he rejoined, "I must; my vows are pledged. Once a priest, always a priest; there is no recall." From this it would seem that Vallance, who was at the bottom of this business, recognised Anglican orders; and Aylmer also continued to do so, for he said, "This renegade Church," meaning the Establishment, "is, after all, a branch not yet finally severed from the parent stock." Then he became a Catholic, and "went into retreat" in a "lonely cell," where he had rather a bad time, and "long strings of Latin prayers" were "imposed on him as a penance." Then he went to sleep in church and dreamt of Agatha. Then he "multiplied prayer and penances," but after seven years "he cast away the fetters that enslaved him," and returned to the Church of England. Very wisely he took "no fixed charge, but preached as an evangelist" whenever he felt inclined.

Rosamund was less fortunate, for a long time she was "nominally a member of the Anglo-Catholic Church," and it was "judged expedient" by her spiritual guides that she should remain so; but finally she "acknowledged the claims of the parent Church," and became a nun at Saint Thérèse, near Rouen. Here her sister went to see her.

"She was quite composed, but very grave, and of course that horrible old nun counting her beads in the background prevented anything like confidence. Just two or three minutes we had, the old lady being suddenly called off guard, and then I put out my hand as far as it would go, and tried to grasp Rosamund's hand, and I said, 'Are you happy? Speak quickly—if you wish to return to us, say so, and Claude and Ralph will manage it.' I could see something like a spasm pass across her thin, wasted features. Then she answered, 'I am content. There can be no change now; it is too late.' 'Only say you repent,' I urged, 'and you shall be free. You are a British subject; they cannot, dare not, detain you against your will.' She only shook her head hopelessly and said sadly, 'Ah, you do not know!' And then Sister Brigida came back, and we could say no more; she evidently understood English. As we parted Rosamund whispered: 'Oh, Gertrude, pray for me! pray for me!' To think of her asking *me*, a heretic, to pray for *her!*'"

"Her brother Claude resolved to pay her an annual visit, and claim her freedom, should she desire it, by an appeal to the British Government;" but she remained in the convent, and for aught I know she is there still.

V. PROTESTANT POETS.

I SAY "poets," because I would not willingly hurt any one's feelings, and I once mortally offended a gentleman by calling him a verse-writer. I fancy he would have preferred to have been termed a pickpocket! Moreover, one of the band, as we shall see later on, proclaims proudly, "I am a poet": and who is more likely to know? So much by way of preface: I now proceed to cull a few of the flowers which adorn the slopes of the Protestant Parnassus.

In the autumn of 1864, a series of letters—in every case anonymous—appeared in the *Daily Telegraph*, regarding the removal of a young girl to Belgium in the care of two nuns. The matter created some sensation, and it was brought before the Town Council of Dover, the place whence the embarkation took place. The mayor then said that "the young person alleged to have been abducted was insane, and that she was being carried to a *maison de santé* at Bruges." There seems to be no doubt that the removal was technically illegal—at least so the Home Office decided: although, "as those concerned appear to have been actuated by no improper motives," no legal proceedings were instituted. This episode forms the subject of a "metrical narrative"—*Sister Theresa, née Ryan, The Abducted Nun*, by James Lord, of the Inner Temple, Esq., Barrister-at-Law, author of *The*

Theory and Practice of Conveyancing, *The Vatican and St. James's*, etc. The special characteristic of this poem is the way in which the author's legal training renders him anxious to be accurate—an unusual feature in Protestant fiction: so that a statement in the text is often qualified in a footnote. Thus, when we read :—

> The train now starts from London Bridge ;
> It soon will Dover reach,
> Where waits " the good ship " *Privilege*,
> Off Dover's shingly beach—

Mr. Lord, conscious that the name of the ship was a tribute to the exigencies of his verse, something being needed as a kind of rhyme to "bridge," tells us in a footnote :—

We have not the name of the vessel, ship, boat, packet, steamer or what not. It is, however, beyond dispute that some sea-going craft did go from one of the Cinque Ports called Dover to a foreign port, Ostend, and that in such sea-going craft some persons did carry away this young lady, against her will, "to parts beyond the seas."

Similarly, the name "Sister Theresa" seems to be a pure assumption :—

> On entering, it seems that she
> Another name assumed,
> As done by most of those within
> A convent's walls entombed.
>
> "Sister Theresa" sounds as well
> And better far than some,
> Who have, through many centuries,
> Been canonised by Rome.

His anxiety for accuracy leads him to attempt to reconcile the discrepancies between the newspaper letters, with amusing results :—

> Now for one moment let us see
>   How stand we as to dates?
> Which of all these who letters wrote
>   Is right in what he states?
>
> The cabman fixes on a date
>   Which clearly coincides
> With the same day and hour at which
>   The nun to Dover rides.
>
> Another gives the day before—
>   See letter of " A. A."—
> And what he saw took place, he says,
>   On the preceding day.

He is not even sure that the nun who was taken from Mile End to Great Ormond Street [1] is identical with the one who was taken from Dover to Ostend; but from this difficulty he emerges triumphantly:—

> If not, then two unhappy nuns
>   Instead of one, we find,
> In something less than two short days,
>   Sore ill, or out of mind.

Moreover, the medical officers of the hospital in Great Ormond Street did not see the invalid during her short stay there, as Mr. Lord tells us, with a sudden lapse into another metre:—

> They did not know—
> They tell us so—
>   Till she had gone away,
> She e'er had been
> That place within
>   A single hour or day.
>
> The first they heard
> Of what occurred
>   Was through the daily press;
> 'Tis what they say,
> So clearly they
>   Afforded no redress.

[1] From Mile End to Great Ormond Street,
  The distance is not great;
Whether three miles, or more or less,
  'Twere bootless here to state.

> From Tuesday, then, to Wednesday night,
>   Where was this hapless nun?
> Who on this point will throw more light,
>   And tell us what was done?
>
> Was she not there a day and night,
>   Or pretty near as long?
> If cabman and "A. A." are right,
>   Are not these doctors wrong?

It was not even clear from the conflicting statements in the newspapers whether those who removed Miss Ryan were nuns. This the conscientious narrator is compelled to admit.

> Two women held her. Whether they
>   Were "Sisters" or were not,
> The story does not clearly say;
>   But they were in the plot.

The appeal for "more light" came somewhat late, for the whole affair, including the letter from the Home Office, had been ended by the middle of November; whereas "it was not till the month of December that any idea of writing this metrical composition entered [Mr. Lord's] mind."

"The good ship *Privilege*" (or whatever its name may have been) seems to have made a bad passage. Who that has crossed the Channel in rough weather will not sympathise with Sister Theresa when

> "Roll over me," she inly sigh'd,
>   "Your glittering waves, O sea;
> Sweep me away in all your pride
>   From those who torture me."

This reminds me of the sufferer under similar circumstances who said: "For the first hour I was afraid I should die, and for the second I was afraid I shouldn't." It is rare, however, that the ship's officers are so sympathetic as the captain seems to have been in this case; their apathy and their imperviousness to

the action of the waves are wont to inflict additional
pangs on the sufferer from *mal de mer*.

> The captain a deck-cabin gave,
> To make her suffering less;
> No doubt he very strongly felt
> To see her deep distress.
>
> . . . .
>
> Now when the vessel reached Ostend
> As in due course it did,

the unfortunate girl was taken to a *maison de santé*
at Bruges, and there the narrative ends. Mr. Lord
pictures her there, "strange to the language that she
hears," and then adds a conscientious footnote:—

This would probably be the case if she were the child of
poor Irish parents. We have not heard of anything contrary
to it; but of course we do not allege all this as positive fact.
If she was the child of parents in a good position of life she
might have known something of the language.

He then goes on to picture the inquiry at the Home
Office, and puts Sir George Grey's letter into rhyme:
after which he appeals earnestly to his Protestant
countrymen to take the matter up:—

> If we're alive
> In Sixty-five,
>   When Parliament shall meet,
> Some one shall stand,
> With "hat in hand,"
>   And, rising on his feet,
> At once shall ask—
> 'Tis no great task—
>   How doth this matter lie?
>   And say the English people wish
>   To "know the reason why."

But alas! no one asked, nor was the appeal to the
Queen[1] ever made; and with an account of the burial

---
[1] Then let us go and ask the Queen
If nothing else is done,
To have the poor young creature seen—
The poor afflicted nun.

of nuns at Derby, the book abruptly ends. This is the more unfortunate because one feels that a great opportunity was missed. However, it is never too late to mend; and I would suggest to the Protestant Alliance that "The Abducted Nun" "sounds as well," to quote Mr. Lord, as either the "Rescued" or the "Escaped": there should be no difficulty in providing some one to adopt this title and invent an appropriate narrative.

Mr. Lord seems to have shared Mr. Silas Wegg's aptitude for dropping into poetry: here are some verses from *The Vatican and St. James's* (1875), the punctuation of which is remarkable:—

> Manning—decked with Foreign titles,
> Scarlet Hat, and scarlet hose—
> He, John Bull would seek to frighten
> Or—to lead him by the nose!
>
> . . . .
>
> Long may She with Queenly graces
> Rule abroad—beloved at home.
> May he know his proper place—is
> Not in England—but in Rome.
>
> We—would set down naught in malice—
> Cannot ask him here to stay
> Where for tens who give him welcome,
> Thousands wish him—well—away.

Those who are acquainted with the works of "The Poet Close" will find in Mr. Lord's literary style a remarkable resemblance to that last of the Lake Poets.

The Betrayal and the Dream, a poem in five cantos, by William Marshall (London: Kensit, 1888), is a new and much enlarged edition of *Rinalpho's Dream*, by the same author (same publisher, 1887). Rinalpho, to whom we are not introduced until the fourth canto, "ruled a parish wide," and got on very well,

Protestant Poets.

> Till his mind, being caught by its sense
> In the exquisite web of the errors of Rome,
> Sank numbed to impotence,
> And lived but over that web to crawl.

In his dream

> He saw his own church table there,
> And the thing that hid with a lie
> Its legs to make it an altar seem
> To the Holy Spirit's eye.
>
> He saw that his altar-cloth's monogram meant
> As heathen alone, not this
> Iesus, Hom., Salvator, but,
> Isis, Horus, Serapis.[1]

Rinalpho saw so many unpleasant things in his dream that

> His agony woke him: a burning fever
> And a three months' illness ensued.

What became of him, we know not; for the poem ends abruptly.

The work is mainly occupied with an exposure of the Jesuits, who, "having slunk to their holes in Oxford," soon came out of them, and made their influence felt. They seem to have been numerous, for

---

[1] This ingenious explanation of the I. H. S. is set forth at length in a delightful article on the subject, full of Protestant erudition, published in *The Protestant Observer* for April, 1898. The writer quotes at length from that extraordinary manifestation of ignorance—I beg pardon, from "that valuable work"—*The Two Babylons*, "by the learned and devout Rev. A. Hislop." "His explanation," says the writer, "is that they refer to the Egyptian triad of deities, Isis, Horus, Seb, the mother, child and father, introduced during the corruptions of Christianity by designing Pagan priests." The writer continues, "Hislop's explanation suits the whole case," but in the next sentence says, "In one point Hislop's conclusion seems doubtful. Seb was not the father of Horus, or husband of Isis. It is, therefore, quite improbable that the S. refers to Seb, as there would be no connection in such a triad. The husband of Isis was Sor-Apis, or Serapis," and "the true original meaning of this mystic monogram, so used by Ritualists, Romanists and Jesuits, is none other than the great Egyptian triad of Isis, Horus, Sor-Apis." We live and learn.

> In pulpit and pew, and at barrack and bar,
>   And in cabin and in court,
> And in senate and shop, and on staircase and road,
>   And on ocean and in port,
>
> The Jesuits long had in every guise
>   Through the country been going about,
> To crumble the oneness of Protestants
>   In order to put them to rout.

Success appears to have attended their efforts so far as "crumbling the oneness of Protestants" is concerned, as *Whitaker's Almanac* for 1896 enumerates no fewer than 291 Protestant sects—an increase of fifteen since the previous year. Mr. Marshall indeed admits that they

> wrought with some effect;
> They won the wealthy by stealth;
> And they bought up the poor with every sort
>   Of comfort by means of the wealth.
>
> They enticed poor children to cheapened schools;
>   And, luring with music the young,
> Made them Papists, and sent them back to their friends
>   As Protestants in tongue.

Nor was this all. As we have heard before in prose, so now we are told in verse how

> the Jesuits filled
> This isle with their agencies,
> Its pulpits and kitchens and drawing-rooms,
>   Its newspaper offices,
>
> Its barracks and clubs and hospitals,
>   Its marts and Protestant leagues,
> There was not one spot in it free from their watch,
>   Or defended from their intrigues.

They were especially successful, strange as it may seem, among the Nonconformists.

> Rome therefore sent Jesuits whither she deemed
>   Were a Goshen of Anglican schism,
> A promised land of Welsh dissent
>   And Scottish Calvinism.

> And the very body-guard of freedom,
>   The Dissenters and Liberal party,
> Received their masters with great politeness,
>   Idiotic, happy, and hearty.

The English people, indeed, were quite blind to these machinations—never was our race represented as so unintelligent as it is in Protestant fiction!—and even admired "the zeal of the priests."

> At length with much awe they a Cardinal saw
>   At the head of their Protestant forces
> In their own defence of their scriptural truth
>   And attack of inebriate courses.
>
> Had the money spent in making men sober
>   By their vowing no spirit to drink
> Gone in preaching them Protestant truth from the Bible
>   They had soberer been, I think.

Yet, if reports be true, the preaching of Protestant truth has not exactly produced this effect in Scotland.

Occasionally the Protestant poet is almost injudiciously candid. One wonders what the admirers of Gavazzi thought of Mr. William Brockie's verses [1] upon the extinction of that Protestant light. I give the first and last stanzas.

> Alas, for Father Gavazzi!
> The pink of orators was he!
> But his glory has waxed dim,
> The saints have discarded him!
> At Manchester, the other week
> Nobody went to hear him speak
> Of any respectability;
> None showed him the least civility;
> Supporter he had none,
> On the platform he stood alone,
> Clean cut by all the great guns,—
> So the newspaper paragraph runs.
>
> . . . .

[1] *The Confessional, and other Poems.* Sunderland, 1876.

> Don't it make your blood run chill, eh ?
> To think first of Father Achilli,
> By that bold renegade Newman,
> To feast the mob inhuman,
> Served up in a way so saucy ;
> And now of Father Gavazzi,
> Turning out, shame to tell,
> A perfect infidel !
> Then there was Rongé [*sic*], poor man,
> Seduced by the Rationalist clan.

The Rev. Dr. Grattan Guinness, who is fully entitled to a place among Protestant poets, has recourse to the meretricious adornments of varied type in order to emphasise his points. Here is his view of the Church :—

> Rome is a HIERARCHY ; and means the reign
> Through priests of the old Enemy again.
> Two hundred millions own the sacred sway
> Of the Triple Tyrant, and his word obey.
> Upon them HALF A MILLION PRIESTS, with feet
> Audacious, tread and tramp as seemeth meet.
> Upon the priests A THOUSAND BISHOPS climb,
> And cluster on their shoulders ; while sublime
> Above the Bishops CARDINALS appear ;
> And over them the ruler of the sphere,
> The AGED AUTOCRAT, and close behind
> Frowns the dark visage of the Master Mind !

"The Master Mind" is, of course, the Jesuits, about whom the Reverend Doctor is very emphatic, and whom he thus apostrophizes :—

> O form half seen, half hidden, black as night,
> And blood-stained, furtive, shrinking from the sight,
> Slippery, unearthly, calculating, cold,
> The Papal Helm and Sceptre Thou dost hold.
> . . . .
> The company of Jesus ! SATAN'S band,
> His own militia ; his material hand,
> His heart of falsehood, his most subtle mind,
> His Serpent Shape, which coil in coil doth wind,
> And in the folds the fangs, the glittering eyes !
> . . . .
> Slip slyly into Palaces and Shrines,
> Sit in confessionals, dig secret mines,

> Plot, plan, pretend, dissemble, darken, lie,
> Heaven yet shall drag thee forth and lift thee high,
> And with its hand of might in holy ire
> Fling thee, foul serpent, in the eternal fire.[1]

Dr. Grattan Guinness's intimate acquaintance with the Jesuits may be inferred from these vigorous lines, but he is kind enough to supply positive proof. Prefixed to this chapter on "The Power behind the Pope" is a picture entitled "The Jesuit Ribera at Rome." This Jesuit, who also figures on the cover of the book, is a Capuchin, with cowl and cord complete! Probably Dr. Grattan Guinness will say that he is a Jesuit in disguise.

Dr. Guinness gives a thrilling account, both in prose and verse, of a visit which he paid to "the Inquisitor" in Rome.

> He was enrobed as a Dominican,
> In yellow-white, a proud and portly man;
> His head was cowled, upon his breast he bore
> A golden cross; his ruddy visage wore
> An angry aspect; furrowed was his brow,
> And firm his mouth; I think I see him now!

Nevertheless he was quite affable to Dr. Guinness. Later on, it is true,

> His voice excited, forth he stretched his hand
> With strength as one accustomed to command;
> His rigid finger pointed straight and far;
> He shook his arm, he stretched it like a bar;

and answered questions

> in a tone
> Becoming the Dominican alone;

but Dr. Guinness, judging from his writings, has very little of the *suaviter in modo*, and his attack upon the Inquisition "within its office grim," must have been

---

[1] *The City of the Seven Hills*, section ii. ch. 5. Nisbet (recent, no date). The capitals are those of the original.

somewhat annoying. When he asked the Dominican,

> Had they the Holy Office at this hour
> In other lands?

I cannot help fearing that the Father yielded to a temptation which must have been present to him throughout the interview, and tried to ascertain how much Dr. Guinness was capable of swallowing.

> He said the Bishops were
> Their coadjutors; none might dare demur;
> "*The Bishops do*," said he, "*in every land
> What we in our authority command.*"

I must not omit an example of the political Protestant poet, and I find one in *The Anglo-Fenian*, by Hibbert Newton, D.D., Vicar of St. Michael's, Southwark, published by Kensit in 1890. Dr. Newton holds in equal abomination Mr. Gladstone, the Liberal Party, the Roman Church, and (of course) the Jesuits; and appears to think that a close connection binds them together. The "Sister Theresa" incident seems to have attracted Dr. Newton's notice; but his account of it (which, although written in the first person, is derived—a footnote tells us—from General Phayre's *Monasticism Unveiled*)—shows none of Mr. Lord's caution, though its conclusion is similarly unsatisfactory:—

> On Convents I could give ye many a fact—
> Proofs will be all forthcoming by-and-bye,
> On many a violent, many a murd'rous act—
> Perhaps an incident may certify
> What comes of some nuns, who for freedom try.
> I saw a ship, close lying to a quay,
> A nun dragg'd thither—"Help," in a wild cry
> She wail'd forth, struggling, screaming all the way.
> As no more heard of her, I've here no more to say.

"The Anglo-Fenian" who gives the title to the

book, is, I think, Mr. Gladstone, although I confess I find Dr. Newton difficult to follow :—

> The Anglo-Fenian is a lamb-like beast,
> Showing three horns—I show the third horn, where
> This Jacobin in Satan's favour leased
> A great " House "—who the lease holds for him there ?
> The atheist—to say more I here forbear,
> For want of space, my limits are so small—
> What doth the third horn typical declare ?
> The Liberal to Jacobinic thrall
> Drives ye—He's liberal : that word atones for all.

Dr. Newton, like other great poets, has suffered from want of appreciation. When he published *The Triumph of Israel and the Fall of Babylon*, "a journalist, writing perfectly in the style of a Jesuit, called it a 'nuisance.'" One of the incidents in the poem, we learn from a note by the author, is the luring of a Jewess into a convent by Julian, a Jesuit. This probably accounts for the journalistic Jesuit's gibes : for, as Dr. Newton says,

> From flowering Eden the most fragrant rose
> If tender'd by an angel, it would be
> The veriest " nuisance " to the devil's nose :

and he adds :—

> The " gospel " is the " nuisance " to the devil's own.

Oddly enough, Dr. Newton's own writings are eagerly perused in infernal circles :—

> I'm certain there is not a word of this,
> That is not spitefully by devils read.
> . . . They look upon this page
> Satiric—they hate satire, as 'tis said,
> If pointed at them—so a war they wage
> Against me—It is good : the devil's in a rage.

I can only give one more specimen of Dr. Newton's verse :—

> Could ye materialise me many a word,
> Each word for a bad epithet, then cast
> At random in a dice-box, there all stirr'd
> Suppose that box to think, and from it pass'd
> By sudden jerk what never should come last—
> Jesuit.

As an example of recent Protestant poetry, I will take "*Rhyme and Reason in Romanism.* For the People of England. Including a Suppositional Address by Saint Peter. By an Englishman." (Partridge, 1896.) The author depicts St. Peter's "suppositional" feelings, could he revisit the earth, and assumes that he would "go weeping back to heaven":—

> Yet not, methinks, before he had assembled
> Hierarchs for speech at which they must have trembled.
> Though we know not the course of such a lecture,
> Some portions of it we may well conjecture.
> His hearers, listening to each solemn word,
> Would surely some such strains as these have heard.

St. Peter begins:—

> In uttering to you these grave admonitions,
> I will be just and fair in my admissions.

And ends:—

> I say, farewell, with true commiseration,
> And strong desire you all may gain salvation.

His general style is that of the English translation of the *libretto* to *Lohengrin*:—

> Of heresy and schism ye accuse them,
> And with anathemas full fierce abuse them.
> But they repel by truth your accusations,
> And you, not they, deserve your fulminations.

I will only give one more extract—one which puts Cardinal Vaughan in his true position.

> Heed not the glamour of a Cardinal—
> Roman ecclesiastic—that is all.
> Our bishops Protestant throughout the land
> Above all Papal functionaries stand.

> The President o' th' Wesleyan Conference
> More honour merits, though of less pretence:
> The Chairman of the Congregational Band
> Is higher than a Cardinal in this land:
> A Moderator Presbyterian
> O'ertops all agents of the Vatican.
> That Card'nals are so pampered in high places
> Is one of our incongruous disgraces.

This, however, is hardly as crushing as a note which appeared in *The Rock* some years since: "The word 'Cardinal' is not recognized at the office of *The Rock*."

Space will not allow me to do more than commend to the notice of the amateur a volume which I was fortunate enough to rescue from "the fourpenny box." Its title-page (on which unfortunately is no date) runs: "Elvinor. A Poem. By W. E. C. Dedicated to Mary Fairlie, (*née*)." I quote this but do not understand it. The poem is well worth the money expended on it. Elvinor was a young lady of wealth, whose property "Father Abnyard"—surely this is something new in names?—was anxious to secure for his convent. So he arranged with the Abbot—of whom he had but a low opinion, for he soliloquized about him as

> a loathsome tool,
> A coward, without intellect,
> A proud and cruel fool—

to seize Elvinor and do her to death.

> As Abnyard ceas'd, the Abbot gazed
>   With admiration deep,
> On him, with exultation did
>   His base heart in him leap.
> But suddenly his visage chang'd
>   To disappointment's hue;
> At length he said, "No rack we have
>   Wherewith this deed to do;
> But thumbscrews, knives, and heating rings,—
>   Alas, no rack have we."
> He spoke and his small eyes shone with
>   Outwitted cruelty.

Abnyard however pointed out that torturing would on the whole answer as well as the rack ; and it did.

Mr. Kensit, who has published much Protestant poetry, as well as works of a less innocent character, is himself the subject of a recent poem " by a London Vicar," written in imitation of " John Gilpin " and issued by the National Protestant League. It begins:—

> John Kensit was a citizen
> Of famous London town
> Who, as a doughty Protestant,

—and still more, I would interpolate, as a purveyor of obscene and indecent literature—

> Had got him great renown.

Mr. Kensit's performances at St. Ethelburga's and at St. Cuthbert's, his correspondence with the Bishop of London, and other events, are duly recorded ; and there is a spirited appeal to the bishops, who are adjured to

> Ask of Gideon
> How Israel now to save.

This seems to be an allusion to the Gideonites—those militant members of the Protestant Alliance who are trained for their evangelical and missionary work by an ex-prizefighter under the Driffield Road Methodist Chapel.[1] The poem ends :—

> And should my Lord of London yet
> Invite John home to tea,
> And grasp his hand in Fulham's halls,
> May I be there to see!

I doubt whether Dr. Creighton is sufficiently satisfied with the result of his former entertainment of Mr. Kensit and his friends to extend to them another invitation.

[1] See *The Sun* for 13th and 14th June, 1898, and a pamphlet entitled *Roughs and Religion*, published at the *Church Times* Office.

Protestant Poets. 145

I must now pass on to one who until his death in 1889 might fairly claim the proud position of Protestant Laureate—Mr. Martin Farquhar Tupper, author of *Proverbial Philosophy* and Fellow of the Royal Society. To *The Rock* and other chosen publications Mr. Tupper contributed numerous outpourings of his genius, fifty of which, "although conscious of having written many more," he reprinted in a little volume.[1] This collection does not include "a famous couple—'The Nun's Appeal' and 'Open the Convents,' which were written at the request of Lord Alfred Churchill, and given to Edith O'Gorman, the escaped nun (otherwise the excellent and eloquent Mrs. Auffray), to aid her Protestant lectures everywhere;"[2] but it abounds in gems.

As seems fitting in a Laureate, Mr. Tupper begins with national lyrics: here is a verse of "'Rule, Britannia!' adapted to these times."

> The Nations, not so blest as thou,
> In Papal darkness blindly grope,
> But never will thy starry brow
> Bow down to idols or the Pope!
> Rise, Britannia! Britannia, rout these knaves!
> Britons never shall be slaves.

And here is a specimen of "'God save the Queen,' with additional stanzas":

> May she our Church secure
> Protestant plain and pure,
> As it hath been.
> So shall our State still be
> Freest among the free,
> Shouting from sea to sea
> God save the Queen.

---

[1] *Fifty of the Protestant Ballads and "The Anti-Ritualistic Directorium,"* of Martin F. Tupper, D.C.L., F.R.S. London: Ridgway, 1874.

[2] *My Life as an Author*, p. 203. By M. F. Tupper. 1886.

It was a stern sense of duty that induced Mr. Tupper to come forward as a champion of "the cause"—

> It is time to be stirring and helping the Right,
> By bearing my Protestant part in the fight,
> It is time to do all that an Englishman can
> By honestly taking my side like a man!

He is conscious that he is the mouthpiece of numbers of his countrymen, and that he "voices," as the newspapers have it, their denunciations :—

> I, then, with the thousands who think in my rhymes,
> Denounce these false priests in these perilous times,
> As spawn of the Serpent, ambitiously vain,
> Such as England has crushed, and will crush yet again!

He makes it clear that he does not condemn the just with the unjust :—

> Ye parish priests of England,
>   The good, the pure, the true!
> These angry rhymes in these fierce times
>   Are never flung at you;
> They only hit the traitorous band
>   That shames your reverend ranks,
> For heart and hand with you we stand
>   To stop their Popish pranks.
> So, clergymen of England,
>   We claim your hearty thanks!

It is the bishops, Mr. Tupper thinks—and here he is at one with the *Church Times*[1]—who are mainly

---

[1] See a remarkable article entitled, "A Warning to the Bishops," in the *Church Times* for 10th January, 1896. After "a black list of misdoings on the part of individual bishops," comes "the unformulated charge that the better laity bring against the present Bench. They pay obsequious and contemptible deference to the opinion of the lawyers, the man in the street, and the *Times* newspaper, and they squeeze the Catholic traditions of the English Church till they can appear obnoxious to no one. The Roman Church and its officers, by comparison, are admired, respected, even though not believed in; the English Church and its officers, on the other hand, are accepted as teachers (?) and despised as guides." Canon Knox Little, in the *Westminster Gazette* for 22nd February, 1896, says their silence is "unspeakably disgraceful. I can imagine no use in bishops unless to be leaders in Truth and Morality. The Anglican Bench—in face of the Divorce Court scandals—is most surely a melancholy spectacle."

to blame for the present state of things. Many a head must have trembled beneath its mitre, did it happen to wear one, when these scathing lines, addressed " To Certain Hierarchs," were read :—

> Ye Bishops! in dignified greatness
>   Laying hands on more Bishops forsooth,
> So careful by lordly sedateness
>   To compromise nothing but Truth,—
> We look to your bench for some vigour,
>   Some strength in this Protestant strait,
> But lo! what a pitiful figure
>   You cut both in Church and in State!
>
> Ah! know but yourselves as men know you,
>   Slumbering and dumb in the dark,
> With infidels eager to show you
>   Their lies of the Flood and the Ark,
> With Jesuits plotting and waiting
>   To seize both your folds and your flocks.
> And Popery heartily hating
>   The heretic Church that it mocks!

Mr. Tupper has small patience with those who ignore the need for reform :—

> O think not, friends, by ostrich blinks,
>   And salves, and soft excuse,
> When evil in the nostril stinks
>   To hide up each abuse ;
> Rather, with firm and wholesome hand,
>   Probe every poison'd sore,
> That heal'd and strong, our Church may stand
>   · In beauty evermore!

But his indignation at ritualism does not blind him to the real source of all its evils :—

> But, Ireland! thou art marked withal; thou worshippest the Beast,
> Thou art infected with the plagues that grow of Pope and priest;
> And though our Church hath dwelt with thee for thrice a hundred years,
> Thou hast not loved or honoured her, but dealt her shame and sneers!

One more extract, and we must pass on. It is not with England's approval that Popery is again lifting its head in our midst :—

> Britain frowns and hectors
>   In honest wrath to know
> So many budding rectors
>   Perverted to the foe,
> And vows she will not stand it,
>   To see the parish priest
> A semi-papal bandit
>   Of the Babylonish Beast!
>
> Shall that Italian Ferret[1]
>   Usurp this Lion-throne
> Which Protestants inherit
>   Through their pure faith alone?
> Shall Popery and its vermin
>   (As bad old times have seen)
> Again infest the ermine
>   Of England and her Queen?

The poet answers these questions in the negative, so for the present we may breathe freely.

At Mr. Tupper's death, his mantle descended upon a lady. During the vacancy in the Poet Laureateship after the death of Lord Tennyson, more than one writer suggested that a woman should be appointed to the post. The Protestant laurel, "greener from the brows of him who uttered" irreproachable anti-Papal sentiments, now adorns the head of Mrs. M. A. Chaplin, of Galleywood, Essex. I confess with shame that her poems were unknown to me until the Catholic Conference at Bristol in 1895, when, as we were leaving the hall, some one gave me a tract which had just been sent to him by post. I was at once struck with the beauty and originality of some verses which it contained — so much so that I read them at the dinner with which the Conference terminated, and even ventured, under their potent spell, a feeble imitation of my own, which received the unexpected honour of publication in the three Bristol papers. It is not

---

[1] Note the playful allusion to Pope Pius IX.—Mastai Ferretti.

every author whose maiden efforts meet with such prompt appreciation; but I ascribe this to the model on which I had formed myself. The verses attracted the attention of Mrs. Chaplin, who wrote to expostulate, couching her letter in terms which showed her to be as great a mistress of prose as of verse. "Though a poet," said the lady, "I am no sentimentalist; I never try to gild gold or smear a thunder-cloud."[1]

Mrs. Chaplin's earlier works are collected into a volume entitled *Chimes for the Times*,[2] with an appreciative preface by the Rev. Lancelot Holland, of "walled-up nun" fame. "She manifests a true insight," says Mr. Holland, speaking out of the fulness of his ignorance, "into what enclosed Romish and Anglican convents really are,[3] and rings a sad peal that must now be sounding forth from many a nun's broken heart:—

> 'Oh, register our births and deaths,
> And bid your Senate give
> The glorious freedom of its jails
> To every nun alive.'"

This verse is from "Convent Bells," which Mrs. Chaplin informs me "has had a greater run than any of [her] leaflets"; for, with that ambition "to write a people's songs" which has inspired other lyrists, her works are largely issued in leaflet form, at 1s. per hundred. Another verse—with its accompanying footnote, which recalls Newman's account of the rumours that attended the building of the Birmingham Oratory —may be cited:—

[1] *Bristol Times and Mirror*, 17th September, 1895.
[2] London: Wileman, 1891.
[3] I hear strange tales from the world at large,
    Of subterranean groans;
    Of chain, and mattress, and iron scourge,
    Cages, and infants' bones!

> No father, and no mother knows
> The depth of our distresses;
> You saw our basement builded,[1] with
> Its coffin-like recesses.[2]

Like many excellent Protestants, Mrs. Chaplin considers that the passing of the Catholic Emancipation Act was a blunder. Here are two verses from "Rome's Tactics":—

> She asked for *toleration*, some sixty years ago,
> She was so *innocent*, she said, 'twas *wrong* to treat her *so*.
> It really seemed a *pity* that England should remember,
> Such trifles as the Smithfield fires, and Guido-Fawke's November!
>
> But *then*—as *now* and *ever*—the woman wore a mask,
> *Apostacy* her *aim* was, to *subjugate*, her task.
> The first she has *accomplished*, the Church *has* gone astray,
> But *subjugation* turns the scale a bit the other way.

The use of italics seems intended to lend an additional force to Mrs. Chaplin's remarks, and imparts a pleasing variety to the printed page. Her indignation is kindled at the "objection which some Christians have against mentioning politics in a

---

[1] "A writer in the *English Churchman* tells how he watched the building of the nunnery near King's Cross, and the basement consisted mainly of cells about the size of an ordinary coffin, and says he is constantly passing, sees plenty of girls go in, but never yet saw a funeral come out."

[2] The late General Sir Robert Phayre evidently thought this arrangement of type insufficiently emphatic. In his pamphlet, *Monasticism Unveiled: The Climax*, he printed the verse thus:—

> No father and no mother knows
> The DEPTH of our distresses;
> You saw our *basement* builded, with
> Its coffin-like recesses:
> You KNOW there comes no funeral
> Without the convent gate;
> You THINK there may be PITS and LIME
> Where INFANTS LIE IN STATE!!

One is inclined to remark that, whether or no "infants lie in state," it is evident that some Protestant poets lie in statement.

place of worship"; are we justified in assuming that she would approve of the practice if carried out by the Catholic clergy in Ireland? Here are two of the stirring verses in which she protests against the objection :—

> Really, brother, you are rousing
> Every bristle I possess ;
> Do you *pray* about your country ?
> Sure a Christian can't do less ;
> If they passed a law to-morrow
> Which would put you in a fix,
> And you told the Lord about it,
> Would you call *that politics ?*
>
> If the Queen might be a Papist,
> If the Pope might rule the Queen ;
> If your cottage and your chapel
> Had a barrier between ;
> If they turned you on the roadside,
> Sold your bed and burned your sticks,
> All to lead you to confession ;
> Would you call *that politics ?*

It does not seem to me, if I may answer the question, that this could be called politics, or even politic ; and it seems an odd method of persuading folk to go to confession.

Mrs. Chaplin, by the way, is an authority on the confessional ; every one will recognise the aptitude and accuracy of the following description :—

> A hole in the wall where an unseen eye
> The sanctities of our homes may spy,
> Where a man of sin in a robe of state,
> Buys and sells at a fearful rate ;
> Buys the thoughts of a maudlin girl—
> Buys the fears of a dying churl—
> Selling his soul with the awful lie,
> Of the *absolution* theory.

The prosaic mind might wonder how the "dying churl" is brought to the "hole in the wall," and might even take exception to the "robe of state;"[1] but it must be remembered that Mrs. Chaplin is a poet, as no one who reads the following verse can doubt:—

> Don't you remember the olden time,
> When priest and faggot were in their prime,
> How *easy* it was to lay their hand
> On one of the Bible-reading band?
> There was ever an *ear* aslant the eye,
> There was ever a low lip lisping by,
> And mother and child alike *confessed*,
> *That* which brought *ruin* upon the rest.

Not only nuns, but their mothers, evoke Mrs. Chaplin's sympathy; with the true poetic instinct, she puts herself in their place and asks:—

> Oh! Where is my beautiful girl to-night,
> "The child of my love and care"?
> She is not strong, and may kneel too long
> In the attitude of prayer.
> The wild winds steal to my slippered feet,
> I hear the tempest whirl;
> Will they put a fire in the convent cell?
> Oh! *where* is my beautiful girl?

Here, again, it might be urged that if the mother cannot keep the wild winds from her slippered feet, it is hardly reasonable to expect the nuns to provide her daughter with a fire in her cell.[2]

The poem ends with the following spirited apostrophe:—

---

[1] Whether the "robe of state" be a hat or a waistcoat seems doubtful; but I think the following verse from one of Mrs. Chaplin's later poems indicates that it is one of the two:—

> Don't go to confession; oh, never make known
> The secrets of others, or even your own,
>   To a man in a clerical hat;
> Take *that*, and his waistcoat, and give him a beard,
> And is he a thing to be kneeled to and feared,
>   And for pardon looked hopefully at?

[2] A similar want of provision of modern appliances would appear to exist in the Royal Navy; it will be remembered that on board H.M.S. *Pinafore* a prisoner was reminded that "no telephone communicates with his cell."

> Oh! Where is my beautiful girl to-night?
> VICTORIA—where art *thou?*
> There is liberty written on every gem
> Which crowns thy regal brow;
> Will ye not utter the final word,
> And hush the nation's throes,
> Turn every convent upside down
> And show us what *God knows!*

Victoria is not, as appears at first sight, the name of the nun, but refers to her Gracious Majesty, who, so far as I know, has not as yet uttered even the initial word, and is probably as ignorant as most of us of the "throes" which the nation so effectually conceals. Whether the Queen would be within her prerogative in turning every convent upside down is, I think, doubtful; and I fancy Mrs. Chaplin must be wrong in supposing that liberty is inscribed on the gems of the royal crown. She is, I fear, subject to hallucinations of this kind; for when I sent her a Catholic Truth pamphlet, she told me she saw "in large print at the top of every paragraph: 'A lie is no sin when it is told in the interests of the Church.'" This was certainly an error; as a matter of fact, such a statement does not appear in any of our pamphlets.

It would appear that her Majesty is singularly blind to the dangers which surround her and deaf to the warnings which Mrs. Chaplin and other writers are inspired to utter.

> The very Throne has bent itself
> To Leo's trampling feet;

and the Pope,

> Who holds Victoria vile,

is treated with altogether too much civility.

> Our fascinated Senators
> Bow gratefully and *smile*

when Leo XIII. pretends a friendly interest in England ; and Mrs. Chaplin, in a fine figure, exclaims :—

> God drive conviction's fire-ships through
> This squadron of pretence !

In her second volume, *Sunlit Spray from the Billows of Life* (1898), Mrs. Chaplin deals still more faithfully with our sovereign's shortcomings. Convents have been getting worse.

> Though a raging thirst devours
> There is never a cup of water "ours":

so say the nuns who speak through Mrs. Chaplin's "clear harp in divers tones": they have to "kneel and beg it for charity's sake,"

> And though in the giving our spirit is wrecked
> We must say it is more than we ought to expect.

(This sounds so like an extract from a Savoy opera that I find myself unconsciously echoing—

> We *must* say it is more than they ought to expect !)

And then the nuns utter their complaint at queenly negligence, and indicate the course of conduct which they would like her Majesty to adopt :—

> All the years of Victoria's reign
> She has never heeded our cry of pain ;
> How we finish our mortal woes
> Nobody sees and nobody knows
> Only the pitiless beings here,
> Who do as they will and have nothing to fear.
>
> Oh if she would but stand alo
> By the grating at which we make our moan,
> Would speak by her laws to the Cardinals proud,
> And frown into silence the Romanist crowd,
> And say as she catches our wailings below,
> " These are dens of iniquity ; over they go."

Yet the Queen does not say "over they go"; on the contrary, the Princess of Wales opens a bazaar in aid of the Norwood Convent. Nor do I think it as strange as Mrs. Chaplin appears to do that her Majesty does not employ the expressive monosyllable with which a trade journal has lately dismissed Dr. Horton's assertion that the press was under the control of Catholics. There is such a thing as queenly dignity, as no one knows better than our present sovereign. Mrs. Chaplin writes:—

> Strange—with all the lights of time
> Focussing upon Rome's deeds,
> That *Victoria* does not write
> " Bosh " upon it, as she reads
> Of "the beneficent moral power at the Vatican." [1]

On the whole, this second volume will not, I think, add to Mrs. Chaplin's reputation. There are good things in it, no doubt—notably a poem which tells how

> For the space of six long weeks or more
> We all did argue with unbated warmth

upon the name of an expected addition to Mrs. Chaplin's family; but I doubt if she ever "will recapture that first fine careless rapture" which marked the earlier volume. Yet the following description of convent life—which subject Mrs. Chaplin may be said to have made her own — would be hard to beat. Having told us that among the deprivations to which nuns are subjected is the loss of an interesting privilege which they enjoyed in the days of their freedom—namely,

> to crown the dear grey heads at home with apple-blossom—

Mrs. Chaplin proceeds :—

> Rome takes them, lures them, beckons them from homes of light and beauty;
> Natural women, with a sense of honour, love and duty,

[1] The last line is said to be a quotation from some utterance of Cardinal Vaughan.

And binding hair-cloth to their hearts, and teaching them with scourges,
She disciplines them into tubes for breathing funeral dirges.

My last quotation from Mrs. Chaplin's works shall be from the ballad to which I have already referred as having been put into my hands at Bristol:—

> Are you weary of the home life
> Bonnie chimney-corner girls?
> Are the younger branches wilful?
> Do the big boys spoil your curls?
> Does there seem no time for study?
> Is the housework never done?
> Do you sometimes wonder, wistful,
> What it is to be a nun?
>
> . . . .
>
> Did your mother make those ruffles?
> Lay them on the window-sill;
> There's a coarse serge on a pallet
> In the convent by the mill;
> Feast your eyes on human faces,
> Fix them firmly in your brain;
> You may look no mortal brother
> Fully in the face again.
>
> . . . .
>
> You will kneel before the altar
> In the church through many a night,
> And go barefoot through the winters,
> If it does not kill you quite;
> Some bald priest will make you tell him
> What you dare not even *think*,
> And a cage below the garden
> Hold you if your mind should sink.
>
> . . . .
>
> Oh, be glad of chimney-corners,
> Bonny girlhood, while ye can;
> God in wisdom made the woman
> Meet to minister to man.
> May you never leave the duties
> Of a precious home undone,
> For the wretchedness of learning
> *What it is to be a Nun!* [1]

---

[1] At the risk of being charged with vanity, I append the verses, written in humble imitation of Mrs. Chaplin, which I ventured to recite at Bristol—justifying myself for doing so by the excellent advice embodied in the concluding stanza:—

> Are you weary of the twaddle
> That these silly people write?

The inaugural meeting of the Nonconformist Political Council held in November, 1898—that at which Dr. Horton announced his startling discovery that the English press was in the hands of Papists— was enlivened by an effusion from Mr. Alfred T. Storey, of Guildford. The poem was considered worthy of publication in the *Daily News*, though I hardly think it could have been submitted to the distinguished *littérateur* whose contributions so often enrich the columns of that paper. It runs thus :—

ONE FIGHT MORE.

There's an evil spirit brewing
That would fetter us once more
With abject superstitions
That our fathers broke of yore.
It is rampant all about us
Having flourished while we slept,
For where it could not freely go,
Insidiously it crept.
It seeks not in the manly way,
To battle with the strong,
But sneaks into the house unseen
And draws the weak to wrong.
Of headship of the family
It recks not in the least,
And in the place of fatherhood
Would plant the wily priest.

The Protestant Woman occasionally enlivens the stern prose which is best suited to the exigencies of

Do you wonder why they print it
If they are not idiots quite?
Do you sometimes lose your patience?
Do you feel as if you'd none?
Do you sometimes wonder, wistful,
Why on earth the thing is done?

Do you feel at times quite saddened
That poor folk are so deluded?
Do you often wish that others
Saw the truth the same as you did?
Do you want to stop the rubbish
They put out in such variety?
I will tell you how to do it :
Join the Catholic Truth Society!

the trying days in which we live by a jewel of verse. For example, here are selections from the impassioned verses [1] which flowed from the pen of "A Protestant G.M.C."—whatever that may be—under harrowing circumstances which cannot be better described than in his own burning words. They are headed "Semper Eadem," which seems inappropriate, as neither the poem nor its preface suggests that the Corporation of Peterborough habitually go to mass :—

Upon reading in the *Peterborough Advertiser* for 27th November, 1897, that the Mayor and Corporation of that city, in their *official robes*, had attended *mass* at the Roman Catholic Church on the previous Sunday, and after the service a collection was made for the support of the Roman Catholic School, my mind was stirred up in astonishment at the supineness of the so-called Protestants of England, to allow their public officials to display their allegiance to a system set up by a foreign potentate in our land, *contrary* to the constitution of our beloved country, and I felt constrained to write the following verses as my humble protest against such God-dishonouring practices :—

To subjugate our country Pope Leo is inclined,
And since the days of Cromwell his tactics are refined,
He now comes very softly with flattery and lies,
And tries to gain his object by Jesuitic spies.
. . . .
And are the men of England so slow to understand,
That if they give the Pope their power God's curse is on our land ;
The Mayor and City Councillors may go to mass in state,
But if they mock the God of heaven they'll find their sin is great.
. . . .
And shall the men of England this system now uphold
To train the poor young children (contributing their gold),
In superstitious mazy path to lead them on to sin,
'Till all the world shut out from sight and the poor nun shut in.

Ye Protestants of England, arise and do protest
Against the black confessional, 'tis virtue's horrid pest,
The wives and daughters of this land beset with such a snare,
Demand your strong protection—demand your manly care!

[1] *Protestant Woman*, March, 1898 (cover): those who buy the bound volume will be deprived of this gem.

By the side of this is another poem "transmitted to us by a lady whose hostility to Popery is not less decided than our [Mrs. Arbuthnot's] own." Mr. Arbuthnot is not aware from whose pen they proceeded, but knows that they were written on reading a speech delivered some years ago, in St. James's Hall, by the Rev. Robert [should not this be Hobart?] Seymour, on the inspection of convents.

It begins well :—

> Men of free England ! will ye tame look on,
> And see your household hearths despoiled of those.
> Who made the light and warmth of that dear home
> Which, heretofore, in sanctity was closed
> From treacherous intruder's stealthy guile ?
> " Home " was a sacred world long time in Britain's isle.

Now I would venture to assert that no one will guess what those were "who made the light," and the rest. *Lambs*, dear reader, *lambs!* As in Ireland—at least, such is the Saxon belief—the pig is made at home in the best parlour, so in England the innocent lamb is domesticated by widows. Hear the poet :—

> Up and be doing ! See ! the widow's home
> The wily fox doth enter, and away
> Bear the poor, silly lamb, enticed to roam—
> To cruel artifice an easy prey.
> Haste to the rescue ! Boldly do and dare ;
> Nor let or scoff or taunt inspire with craven fear.

Later on however it appears that this lamb is an alligator—I mean an allegory—and represents a nun, whose pitiable lot is thus portrayed :—

> The convict's cell, the maniac's drear abode,
> The gloomy mine, the toiling factory—
> Inquiry's light on these has been bestowed,
> While woman's fate in darkness hid may lie,
> Within those walls, whose bolts and bars declare
> No secret shall pass out that ever enters there.

Another powerful convent poem, signed "Douglas Russell," appeared in *The Protestant Woman* for December, 1897. It appears that a young lady became a nun, much to the grief of her white-haired parents, who sat staggering round the fire at Christmas, listening to a dismal knell which was heard (apparently at the same time) in a convent cell. So far it is plain enough, but the next verse is too much for me :—

> Two sisters love their manly brother,
> In love most true, his heart responds;
> But all this eve, long for another
> Who cannot join them—she's in bonds!
> What fate is this—Satanic, fell!
> That holds her in a Convent Cell?

Mr. Russell concludes his poem with the customary —and fruitless—appeal " to her who sits on England's throne"; but his phrasing is ineffective compared with that of " M. H. B." in *The Protestant Woman* for June of the same year, which I reproduce in full, mainly on account of the loyal sentiment of the last two lines, which gives a pleasing finish to my chapter :—

> Victoria! Queen! to hearts so dear,
> Her suffering subjects love to cheer:
> She wishes ev'ry step that's ta'en
> To celebrate her "Diamond" reign
> Should be benevolent and kind,
> Charact'istic of her noble mind;
> Oh that she would remember those
> Whose sorrows massive walls enclose
> And cause that o'er Britannia's shores
> All convents should have open doors.
> If lives therein are pure and bright,
> Why shrink to bring them to the light?
> But if those walls hide cruel deeds,
> To open them the greater needs;
> Then maidens longing to be free
> Could taste the joys of Jubilee,
> And louder still the welcome sound—
> "God save the Queen!" shall echo round.

www.ingramcontent.com/pod-product-compliance
Lightning Source LLC
Chambersburg PA
CBHW020304170426
43202CB00008B/495